The Awakening of the Soul:

Spiritual and Psychological Dimensions of Awareness

Dale Noelting, Ph.D.

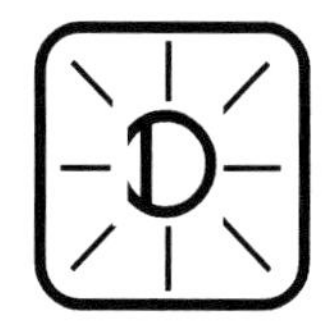

Daylight Publishing
Sewickley, Pennsylvania, USA

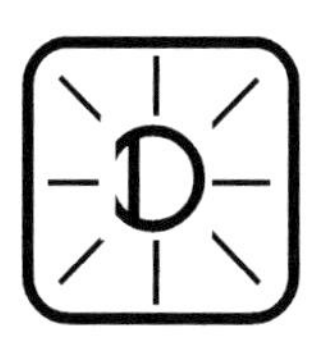

Daylight Publishing
301 Ohio River Blvd., Suite 304
Sewickley, Pa. 15143

Copyright ©2002 by Dale Noelting, Ph.D.

www.dalenoelting.com

All rights reserved. This book may not be reproduced in whole or in part, or transmitted in any form, without written permission from the publisher, except by a reviewer who may quote brief passages in a review; nor may any part of this book be reproduced, stored in a retrieval system, or transmitted in any form or by any means electronic, mechanical, photocopying, recording, or other, without written permission from the publisher.

LCCN 2002090669

ISBN 0-9718179-0-1
1. Personal Growth. 2. Psychology. 3. Spiritual Life. I. Title

First Printing, May 2002
Printed and bound in the United States of America

Contents

Acknowledgments

I would like to thank my readers and reviewers for their helpful comments and feedback on the manuscript. Those people are Dr. JoAnne Jordan, Dr. Thomas Calhoun, Dr. Milton Seligman, Joann Cohen, Deborah Jaybee, Janice Carlino and Susan Danneman.

Much thanks to Daryl Muzy for his support, document design and graphic arts for the book cover. A special thanks to Andy Russell for the magnificent painting that graces the front cover of this book.

A very special thank you to my wife, JoAnne, for all her encouragement and support throughout the lengthy process of writing this book (even though I once overheard her saying, "I'll be happy to have my husband back").

Preface

In the 1960's Abraham Maslow, a psychologist, created a model for human development with a theoretical "pyramid of human needs." The pyramid consists of six levels of needs. The bottom level being basic physiological needs such as food, air and temperature. The second level is stimulation needs such as sex, activity and exploration. The third is safety and security needs. The fourth is love and belonging needs. The fifth is self-esteem needs. The sixth is self-actualization. Maslow stated that we must satisfy each need before we can move up to the next one. Self-actualization is defined as the constant striving of an individual to fully achieve their true potential through personal growth in order to become a more complete human being.

Throughout history there have been individuals and groups that have attained this highest level. However, I believe that for the first time in the history of humankind on this planet we, as a world, have the ability to basically achieve the lower level needs to the point of where a critical mass can be reached. For example, for a large number of people on this planet, food, shelter and clothing needs have been met. We, as a planet, also have the means to alleviate these problems for those who do not yet have these needs met. A significant portion of the world's population is no longer needing to hunt daily for food and toil so hard for the basic necessities of survival that no time is left for anyone to even discuss an idea such as self-actualization. I am not saying that there is no hunger in the world. I am saying that I believe we are at an unprecedented place in the history of mankind. The very fact that you are reading this book adds credence to this viewpoint.

This suggests that our purpose on this planet is not just to survive, but rather to thrive. For many years the arguments have raged over the issue of nature (genetics) versus nurture (environment) and which one controls our destiny. In computer terminology we could describe the environment as being the software or programs. We could view genetics as being the hardware or characterize it as being hardwired in. Given the present work that is being done on the mapping of DNA and cloning, one day this hardware itself may be changeable. At the very least however, software can be changed. We can reprogram the software. We can reprogram ourselves.

How do we reprogram ourselves and remove the blocks that are preventing us from achieving our full potential? How do we create change in our life that brings greater happiness and satisfaction to our selves and those around us? How do we construct a world built on love, trust and goodwill toward others? My hope is that this book will provide one step along that journey. It is a journey of self-rediscovery, and this book is a practical guide to help with that goal. This book will never be complete. It will always be a work in progress because each and every day some new piece of knowledge is obtained or experienced that could add to it. Another piece of the puzzle is found. So this book is a state of the union, in it's truest sense. It is the state of our spiritual union.

I see my goal as nothing less than helping to create a heaven on Earth. Is that goal challenging? Yes, it is. Is it impossible? No, it is not. I am not so naïve as to think that this book alone can bring about the changes I dream of for this world, but I do feel a need to do my part. This book is one step toward carrying out that goal. Yes, I realize that I am simply a drop in the bucket, but I know which bucket I want my drop to be in. Having said that, I do not believe that I am alone in my thinking. I believe that we are on the verge of a major consciousness shift on this planet. I believe that a spiritual awakening is dawning that will change life on this planet forever. It is the spiritual birth of all humankind on Earth. It is the time when all will come to realize that we are all one.

An old proverb says: **"Give a person a fish and you feed him for a day, teach a person to fish and you feed him for a lifetime."** This concept clearly applies to this book. Writing this book is my way of helping to teach others how I have learned to fish. I have been fishing this way for many, many years and have found that it satisfies my hungry and wanting. I have also used the principles and concepts outlined in this book for numerous years in my private practice in psychology with very positive results. I believe this book provides tools that can assist you to find *your* truth. If I can give you one piece of advice as you read this book it is this: apply, apply, apply. Learning how to fish for your self takes the application of knowledge. Knowledge without application is just information. Knowledge with application creates wisdom. Do not just read the book. Make it an experience. Act the book. Live the book. I do not expect, and would not advise, that you blindly accept what is presented here. I do, however, suggest that you examine it, explore it and decide if it is true for you.

This book is most useful as an application tool. Find a behavior, a thought process, an attitude, a belief system or any aspect of your life that you want to change. Then find the tool in the book that would seem to serve you best in achieving that change. Apply the tool and create the targeted change or goal. If you do not have something that you want to change right now, that is okay, you probably will by the end of the book.

What this book offers is more than just solutions to problems. It presents information that can be applied from a spiritual point of view. It solves and averts problems by using this spiritual viewpoint. That is why I refer to them as SOULutions. When these SOULutions are applied they enable us to achieve new heights of awareness, truthfulness, understanding and compassion. They can help us to recognize that we are much more than carbon/oxygen-based life units and can guide us to greater spiritual connection with all beings and God. This universal spirituality I refer to as the UniverSOUL.

This book is written with the idea in mind that it can be applied by individuals in their daily life, as well as by therapists in counseling rooms. One of my primary goals was to bring together the spiritual/religious aspect of who we are, into a synthesis with the psychological. You will notice that the chapters get smaller as you move through the book. That is because what you learn in the first chapter on "I" can also be applied to the next two chapters "We" and "Us". What you learn in the second chapter, "We", can be applied to the third chapter, "Us".

This book is a presentation of information that is primarily conveyed in practical phrases. There is a reason for this. Phrases are precise, concise and easy to remember, especially when we are caught in a moment of difficulty, trauma or emotionality. This makes them particularly easy to recall and apply during those times. I have always been amazed at how powerful and life-changing a simple phrase can be when it is applied to our lives. Secondly, application creates a practice effect. The more you practice them the easier they are to remember and apply and therefore, the greater impact they will have in changing your life.

Be prepared. As you read this book you may experience or become conscious of an expanded awareness of yourself and your relationship with a higher universal order, and you may never be the same again.

I welcome you and hope you enjoy the journey.

Dale C. Noelting
Sewickley, Pennsylvania
May 2002

chapter one

"I"

Frequently I ask clients if they view themselves as a body, a body with a spirit or a spirit with a body. I believe that we are spiritual beings and this body we have is just a vehicle. A vehicle for functioning in the physical world. The body is the chess piece that we move around on the chessboard that we call life. The whole world is our chessboard. Put another way, all the world is a stage and we are but players.

This view helps serve to explain the phrase that "we were created in God's image." I was confused as to which one of us God looked like. I used to wonder whether it meant God was short or tall, young or old, blue eyes or green, Catholic or Protestant, male or female. The quote did not make sense to me. Rather, it did not make sense until I fully realized that we are spiritual beings. We are not our bodies. We are spiritual beings and therefore, are created in God's image.

The Illusion of Death

How foolish we think it would be if an alien came down to our planet saw a car driving down the street and said, "What funny looking beings. They are made of metal, plastic and glass and have four, black, round legs that roll along the ground". We would say, "that isn't us, that's just a vehicle. It's something we use to transport us from place to place." Similarly, the body is a vehicle, just like a car. We get a car, use it to transport us from place to place, but after a while it wears out. For a number of years we are able to replace or repair some of the parts, but eventually it deteriorates to the point of where it ends up in a junkyard. We even hear people say at times that the car finally died on us. Similarly, we get a body, we use it to transport us from place to place, but after a while it wears out. For a number of years we are able to repair and even replace some of the parts, but eventually it deteriorates to the point of where it ends up in a graveyard. Just as we are not the car, we are not the body. The car dies, but we do not. The body dies, but we do not. We are eternal. The human spirit continues on…as we were in the beginning, are now and ever shall be. There is only physical death. Death is just the name given to the beginning of the point in time when the illusions of the physical world end. Death is not the end of our life; it is just the end of this particular lifetime.

Arguments have raged about the point at which life begins for a fetus. We may find in the near future that a legal determination may be made on this question. We may see it being defined as when the spirit enters the fetus (when this is finally able to be measured or determined). It is also possible that stillborn babies and some miscarriages may be fetuses that have not, or not yet, had the spirit enter them.

Similarly, there are many cases of people being in the hospital on life support. In some of these cases the person has no brain waves and is considered to be "brain dead." We may eventually discover that in these cases; the spirit has left the body.

An Awakening

Gaining full recognition of our spirituality is like being reborn. Many associate a sense of being reborn or born again with Christian religion. That is only one example of it. The rebirth or born again experience is, in essence, an awakening. It is achieving a new level of awareness about oneself, one's place in, and connection to, a higher level of what one may call the universe, God or a related term. It may be attained, for example, through a religion, spiritual growth, or meditation. It can be a profound spiritual illumination of that which has appeared to be, or was, hidden. It brings about a transcendence and a sense of oneness and awe. It is a feeling of having one's eyes opened for the first time and then experiencing the world in a way that is different and more expansive than one's previous viewpoint. Some may call it an epiphany. It has been said that unless a man be born again he cannot see the kingdom of God. This transformation, or rebirth, is an act of change that begins and occurs when a person moves from the viewpoint of seeing oneself as a physical person who is having a spiritual experience to knowing oneself as a spiritual being who is having a physical experience. So, as described by that well-known troubadour of our times, Bob Dylan, "He not busy bein' born is busy dyin'." That being the case, let's get busy bein' born.

Certainly, those who wish to do so, can continue to play the game of life the way they have been. They can choose to believe that they are not an actor on a stage that is playing a role. They can even defend their right to be less conscious. But when they do, they are actually signing a contract to play the role of the puppet in the next scene of their dark play. They are choosing to be unaware of who they really are and operating from the physical world, rather than the spiritual world. As a result, their mind and ego will be sitting in the director's chair. "No lights. Camera. Action."

Plato declared that, "Those who have once begun their heavenward pilgrimage may not go down again to darkness and the journey beneath the earth, but they live in light always."

Some people claim to see a light surrounding a person's body. Most refer to it as an aura. This aura or light surrounding the body seems to be a manifestation of the spirit. It appears to be the light of the spirit. This may also be the same light and energy that is detected around the body by Kirlian photography. The process developed by Senyon Kirlian in the 1930's found halos of light and bursts of light energy surrounding the body and body parts like the hands. Note, however, that this light is outside of, and bigger than, the body. This suggests that the spirit is not contained within the body, but in actuality is the reverse. The body is contained within the spirit.

The Spiritual versus the Physical (STEM) World

I believe that there may be numerous levels or wavelengths to this light or energy, just as an onion has ever-enlarging layers upon layers. The strongest, brightest or most dense and noticeable are closest to the body. This is because we choose to center ourselves there. This is where we place our focus and where we assume our primary viewpoint as a spirit. We could also call it our sightpoint or anchor point. The further we move away from this anchor point around the body the fainter and less perceptible our wavelengths or lightwaves become. I suspect that these layers of ourselves are so great and far-reaching that they encompass all that exists. It encompasses all Space, Time, Energy and Matter, which I refer to with the acronym STEM. STEM are the components that make up the physical world.

If our true nature is that we exist simultaneously in all periods of time (past, present and future) and at all places in the universe, then you exist in present time at this very moment and in this precise place (reading this book) because that is the viewpoint you choose. Since you exist everywhere you are able to assume other viewpoints of your choosing.

Keep in mind that when I say that we exist in all periods of time that I am speaking in physical terms. It is our physical bodies and the physical world that are anchored in to past, present and future times. At the highest level of our soul, The UniverSOUL, time does not exist (because matter does not exist). Physicists say that you cannot have matter without time, nor time without matter.

Is all of this a fact? Yes, I believe it is. It just has not yet been proven. Just as the world was round prior to Columbus and the other early ocean explorers discovering that the world was round. The fact that it hadn't yet been proven did not make it less of a fact. It was simply that the world was unaware of the fact. It went against the popular belief and when proven true it completely reversed the accepted and commonly held world beliefs. I believe that is what will happen in regard to our spiritual nature. What seems incomprehensible today becomes incontrovertible tomorrow. English philosopher, John Locke stated, "New opinions are always suspected, and usually opposed, without any other reason because they are not already common." It would probably not be too extreme to state that the most ignorant type of ignorance occurs when an individual opposes or dismisses something which they know nothing about.

Our true nature is a spiritual being. Our true nature is a limitless soul, free from the constraints of STEM. Imagine an upside down letter "T" (see Chart 1, Viewpoints of the Soul). The juncture where the two angles meet is present time. The horizontal plane is what we experience as a physical body moving through the past and present towards the future. It is the world or existence that the majority of people would describe as being "life".

The upright part of the upside down "T" would be the vertical level or plane. The lowest level of this vertical plane would be at the juncture where it meets the horizontal plane. At this level the person perceives himself as a body and fully exists in the STEM world (the horizontal plane). This level could be called "body without recognition of the soul". The next level up could be called "body with recognition of the soul". The highest level on the vertical plane could be called "soul that is operating a body". Each of these levels contains many, many sub-levels. You can get a general idea of where people are at by asking them if they see themselves as a body, a body with a spirit or a spirit with a body.

As a "body without recognition of the soul" we create and experience our reality on a horizontal level or plane as we move through the physical world, which is why STEM exists for us. The STEM world is our lowest level as a spiritual being. It is as completely in the physical world as we can get. Do not think that the physical world has no use. It can be beautiful. The physical world is a place to express who we are and to explore who we can become.

Recognize also, that I am not saying that those who view themselves as a "body without recognition of a soul" are lower level beings. It is more accurate to say that they are simply operating from a lower level viewpoint.

I am in no way making or passing judgments on their beingness. We all have the same nature and potential.

We can also experience our reality on a vertical plane, as we operate more from a spiritual viewpoint and less from a physical world point of view. All beings have energy that has a wavelength and a frequency. I believe that as we grow spiritually our vibrational level changes. It increases to a higher vibrational rate. As we vibrate at a higher rate we are also less affected or influenced by time and by all of STEM.

If you view the world as a threatening, fearful, unhappy place and you allow yourself to be at the mercy or the effect of everything around you, and you wish it was not that way, then you are operating at a lower vibrational rate and level. If, however, you are choosing to view the world as a happy, interesting, exciting, non-threatening place, then you are allowing yourself to be cause over things around you. You are then operating from a higher vibrational rate and level.

We have probably all had experiences of anger and rage. When we do this we can actually feel our bodies get more tense and stiff. We may actually even feel heavier and may feel an urge to get more physical and possibly throw something or hit someone or something. Conversely, when we are experiencing joy or love we often feel lighter. We may even feel that we are almost floating. This is because anger, rage and fear are emotions that are associated with the physical world. They are emotions that are more solid and body-oriented. At the lower vibrational levels we are putting more of our attention, focus and viewpoint in the physical world. As we focus our viewpoint in the physical STEM world, we become more dense because we are more compressed, more consolidated and more condensed.

When we experience love or joy, for example, we move up vertically, and shift out further from the physical world, becoming less attached or anchored to it. That is because these emotions belong more to the spiritual world. At these higher vibrational levels we are more spread out, more dispersed and more expanded.

The STEM world, and our bodies, seem to become more real to us at a lower vibrational level. It makes the physical world more solid and appear more real. Unfortunately, the more real and solid the physical world becomes, the more we get away from the truth of our true spiritual nature. We become stuck in the illusion of the role we are playing and begin to mistakenly perceive the stage set as the real world. It is important to recognize that we are not a surgeon, a secretary, an electrician, a store clerk, a beautician or a psychologist. These are roles. We are spiritual beings. We are spiritual beings who have lost sight of the fact that we are spiritual beings. This lack of awareness, however, is undergoing a change and I believe that very shortly we will achieve a worldwide acknowledgment of our true spiritual nature as an accepted and unquestioned fact.

The UniverSOUL

When we are coming from the highest level of who we are as a spiritual being we are at our most expanded. At our greatest expansion we are most acutely aware of our connection to and our union with all other souls. When we operate from this vibrational level, we are the universal soul. I call this the UniverSOUL.

One measurement of the degree to which an individual is on the UniverSOUL level can be determined by the number of viewpoints that being can assume.

These can be viewpoints at any place in the universe or the viewpoints of other beings. This does not mean that you have to agree with every viewpoint that you are able to assume. It does mean, however, that you can see it from that other perspective. You attempt to understand it based on their history and circumstances. If you can assume the viewpoint of another individual and understand the reason for their words and behaviors you are beginning on a vertical path. Again, this does not mean that you necessarily agree with that viewpoint, just that you understand it. If you can do this with many individuals then you are clearly a vertically traveling being, especially the more divergent their viewpoint is from your own. When you are able to do this with all beings then you are functioning on a UniverSOUL level.

How do we go about achieving these higher levels of beingness? First, we begin by recognizing that there are only two primary emotions: love and fear (the yin and yang). Every other emotion can be subsumed under one of these two categories. Try it and see under which one would we categorize hate or embarrassment? At the core of hate is usually fear that the person or thing may harm us in some way. Embarrassment can be described as the fear that something we have done will be perceived by another person as an indication that we are incompetent or stupid. Where would we categorize joy or admiration? Obviously under love. Fear is primarily negative and physical. Love is positive and spiritual. The more that we are able to operate from a viewpoint of love the higher our vibrational rate becomes.

Our Slumbering Consciousness

We need to awaken from our slumbering consciousness. The world is basically daydreaming. We are sleepwalking through the world (the physical world) believing that it is reality. We will even adamantly prove it to anyone who questions it by banging on a table with our fist and asserting, "See that's real…that's reality." Too often we look, but we do not see. We listen, but we do not hear. Awakening from the dream is paramount. Norman Mailer wrote, "There is a law of life so cruel and so just, which demands that one must grow or else pay dearly for remaining the same." Let's all make a choice to love and grow.

If we wish to seek peace and love in the world then we not only have to give it out, but encourage others to create and send it out as well. In order to get others to send it out, start by sending it to them so that they can begin experiencing it. As employers, for example, treating employees with love, respect and caring, and allowing them to have peace on their jobs is a priority. The same guideline applies in our homes and in our social situations. We can do it with our families and neighbors, our communities, towns, cities, states and countries. This is the only way to truly attain peace on earth. We cannot achieve peace on earth if just one of us wishes it. But if we all express this wish and create it, then we connect up a network of people who have the same belief. When the very last person is given, and has received and attained, peace and love, then it will exist as a planet. We will have created heaven on earth. **Heaven on earth will be a place where each soul can live in love and can become all it is capable of being.**

As an aside, I have always found it interesting that we perceive heaven (the spiritual) as up and hell (the physical) as down. We see the ground and earth as dense, physical and compressed matter. We see the heavens as expanded and expansive. This view aligns with the view of our vibrational levels.

In his early studies of the mind, Sigmund Freud, studied two components that he described as the unconscious (now more frequently referred to as the subconscious) and the conscious. We could describe the conscious mind as the part of the mind we can perceive of, and of which we are aware of the mental processes that are taking place. It is the component of our awareness that is capable of being perceived by an individual at any given moment. Our subsconscious could be presented as the part of our mind that contains drives, urges, mental images and processes that are below our level of awareness and not under our willful or voluntary control. However, through growth-oriented actions and insights we are capable of making these unconscious components conscious.

There is a third level of awareness that is now being spoken of and written about. This is the superconscious. It is the part of the mind that is generally above our level of awareness, but which can be accessed. We are able to access this when we are functioning at our highest levels of beingness. We can also access this, for example, through practiced meditation, deep prayer and hypnosis.

One of the problems we have in attaining higher levels of beingness is that we have unconscious and conscious thoughts, feelings, impulses and behaviors working against this goal. Sometimes we are fully conscious, and at other times semi-conscious, of the fact that we sabotage achieving our highest goals. In other situations we are completely unaware that we are subverting our goals. In fact, if someone suggested during these subversive situations that we were sabotaging our self, our goals, or our situation, we would very likely vehemently deny it. To begin to achieve higher levels of beingness and break free from these constraints we can start by understanding how our mind operates.

What are the reasons we would sabotage our own life, liberty and happiness? There are numerous possibilities. It might be because we have two or more competing purposes and therefore have opposing goals (which is described in detail later in the book). We could be basing our words or actions on inaccurate knowledge or misinformation. We may be responding to a stimulus in the present based on some similar past response to a similar past stimulus. An example of this last situation would be if an adolescent was beaten up by another adolescent who was big and had a muscular physique, so that as an adult in present time he now avoids men who work out or do body building. Imagine that one of our present time goals is to make friends and get along with people. At the same time we avoid a person who has never harmed us, but simply reminds us of someone from our past. As a result, we lose what potentially might have been a wonderful friendship.

I ask you to bear with me for the next dozen pages as I explain the theory on which much of the book is based. The concepts of the UniverSOUL Library, triggers and WEBSATs could all be explained in one example, but it would then become so convoluted that it would be confusing and difficult to understand. So, I have chosen to present each individually. Even though there will be some repetition I believe it will be time well spent. These are important concepts to grasp because they lay the foundation for the ideas and tools that are introduced. Also, the more thoroughly these concepts are comprehended the more you will fully understand exactly how much impact they have in your own life.

Trauma Creates Drama

How do we stop sabotaging our lives on both conscious and subconscious levels? First, we begin by understanding the impact that the mind has over our lives. The memory of each event, experience and trauma in our lives is not only filed in our mind or memory banks, but is also cross-filed under each component, aspect, or detail of each memory. The ultimate goal is to be able to remember a traumatic situation from our past without having to relive it. When we do relive it we can get very dramatic, and at times, we can even become overly dramatic and extremely emotional about it. **Trauma creates drama.**

It can be productive if the past is used as information and for gaining awareness. If the past is used or experienced as a way to remain stuck, to be a victim or to not learn from our mistakes, then it is not only useless, it is certainly unhealthy.

The Spiritual Library and Memory System

Remember also that our mind is not our brain. Our brain is the approximately three pounds of gray matter that is part of the central nervous system and is contained within our cranium. The mind on the other hand is a storage and control system.

As a storage system the mind is like an immense library with hundreds of thousands or millions of books. Some are full-length novels and some are short stories. Everything that has ever happened to us is in these books. Our mind is constantly recording, categorizing and cataloging every detail of every event that occurs to us. It never shuts down. When we are asleep or unconscious and have no conscious memory of what occurs the recording still goes on, but is filed in the subconscious mind. Even when we are in the womb, prior to birth, the recording is taking place. All of this information is filed and cross-filed.

To explain it more fully let's say, for example, that a traumatic event occurs to me. I'm driving down a winding country road with a friend on a sunny summer day at about twelve o'clock noon in a blue sports car. Another driver doesn't stop for a stop sign and pulls out in front of me resulting in a two-car accident. The whole event and all the details would be catalogued in one book in the mind. In addition, every component of the trauma would be cross-filed. These would include any words, emotions, behaviors, sensations, attitudes and thoughts, as well as the physical aspects such as people, places, things and time. Imagine that the books in our mental library are all loose-leaf books. Each book is organized along a time-line that begins with the earliest event first and ends with the most recent event. So we would add, for instance, a write-up of this event and place this page in the back of the book titled "Automobile Accidents." If there was not already a book with the title a new book would be started.

If I displayed anger in front of my friend at the other driver who caused the accident then that would also be filed and cross-filed. So we can imagine it being filed in a somewhat thick book titled "Anger." This book would contain every angry situation I was involved in or that I observed. It would contain every angry situation that I caused to myself or another person, that another caused to me, or that another caused to another that I was aware of or that I had observed.

In addition to the thicker book titled "Anger" the event would be filed in a less thick book titled "Anger With Another Person Present." It would also be placed in a thinner book titled "Anger Due To A Car Accident With Another Person Present." Other books the incident would be cross-filed in might include Incidents At Noon, Incidents With Stop Signs, Incidents With Screeching Tires, Incidents With Pain, Incidents Of Fear, and so on.

Each book would become a chronological listing of that particular aspect of the event along with all previous similar aspects or events that would fall into that book title. Of course, each incident in each book would contain all the rest of the details of that specific incident.

Picture the filing system as being like a completely detailed description of the incident typed onto one page. Then imagine making hundreds of copies and filing one copy each into every loose leaf book with a title that contains any aspect at all of the incident.

The spiritual library system would be structured in levels in the following way. Each page would be a detailed account of one particular incident. This page (i.e., incident) would be Level One. Level Two would be each specific book title, such as "Anger." Level Three would be every book that we have accumulated from our experiences in this lifetime. Level Four would be every book from every one of our lifetimes. Level Five would be every book from every lifetime of every being. I refer to Level Five as the UniverSOUL Library.

How does this library of information affect us? Well, imagine that I'm walking down Sixth Street at midnight and a man grabs me and pulls me into an alley. He puts a gun to my head and demands money. Suppose the man was average height and build. He had on a black hat, glasses, beard and mustache, blue shirt and brown pants. What would I be thinking and feeling? I might have an urge to fight him or possibly to run ("fight or flight"). I may be thinking, "Why Me, I'm a nice guy?" My heart rate would likely be higher, my body temperature would be increased and my palms would begin to sweat. I may be feeling anxiety, anger, resentment and fear. Now all of these feelings, thoughts and bodily reactions are associated with this incident. Also associated with it are the time (around midnight), the location (Sixth Street), the description of the robber and the gun, as well as an alleyway, brick walls, a couple of banged up trash cans, and anything and everything that can be recorded by my five sense organs. Therefore it covers all smells, tastes, touches, sounds and sights. Of course, this event is recorded in full detail and then filed as a page in all the appropriate memory books.

The Triggering of WEBSATs

Let's now say that it's a week after the original incident of being robbed. I am again walking down Sixth Street at midnight (hey, I never said I was smart) and a man is walking toward me of average height, average build and is wearing a blue shirt and brown pants. He's wearing a black hat, glasses and has a beard and mustache. What do you believe I might be thinking and feeling? If you said an increased heart rate and an urge to flee, you would probably be right. I also might have any or all of the Words, Emotions, Behaviors, Sensations, Attitudes or Thoughts that were in the original incident. (I use the acronym WEBSAT in place of this string of words describing the possible associations). This re-experiencing occurs because a trigger goes off…a switch gets thrown and I have the conscious thought, "That looks like the man who robbed me." Then I mentally go back in time to my memory of the event a week ago and I pick up *any or all* of the WEBSATs and come back into present time re-experiencing them to some degree.

Now let's change it slightly. Picture that it's a week after the original incident and everything is as stated in the paragraph above except that now the man doesn't have the hat on. Do you believe I would still have the conscious thought, "That looks like the man who robbed me?" I believe I would. The recognition factor might be very slightly reduced, but I would still have the thought. So the trigger would go off and I would react with any or all of the WEBSATs from the original incident.

Let's again say that it's a week after the original incident and I'm walking down Sixth Street and I see a man who seems to perfectly fit the description of the robber except that now he doesn't have the hat on and he has black pants on instead of brown. Would you expect that the trigger would go off for me? Yes, it would. The recognition factor might be slightly more reduced, but it would still set off the trigger. The trigger goes off and I go back in time picking up any or all of the WEBSATs and re-experience them.

Now let me cut to the chase. What I'm going to do is keep describing scenes one week after the original incident. I would make them similar to the original incident except for the fact that I would keep changing aspects of the second event making each event more and more dissimilar to the original incident of a week earlier. I would change the robber's shirt, take away his mustache and then his glasses. I'd add or take off ten pounds of his weight. Keep in mind that the more dissimilar each event is to the original event then the more it would reduce the recognition factor. I would change other aspects too, such as the time of day. Instead of midnight I would make an incident 10pm, then 6pm, then 12 noon. Instead of Sixth Street I would change the street to 8th Street, then 40th Street, then across the state, then across the country. I would keep reducing the similarities to the original incident, and therefore the conscious recognition factor, until you felt I would not have the conscious thought, "That looks like the man who robbed me."

Maybe the second incident would occur six months later when I'm across the country walking in a park. It's 12 noon, and the robber walks toward me. He has no hat, glasses, beard or mustache. He's wearing a Hawaiian shirt, shorts and has put on five pounds since the week before. Would I have the conscious thought, "That looks like the man who robbed me?" No, I probably wouldn't. So does that mean the trigger wouldn't go off? You would probably say, "Yes, it wouldn't go off." However, you might be forgetting one thing. We don't just have a conscious mind with conscious thoughts. We also have a subconscious mind at work. The information from our senses would be fed into our subconscious mind, just as it is fed into our conscious mind. The difference is that we are unaware of any thoughts that take place in our subconscious mind. So when the trigger goes off, after the information from our senses is received on a subconscious level, we are unaware that the process even took place except that we do begin experiencing the WEBSATs that are restimulated.

Imagine that you are walking down a street, occupying the conscious mind, thinking that on the way home tonight you have to remember to get bread, milk and stop by the dry cleaners. What you are not *consciously* aware of, since you are occupying the conscious mind and have much of your attention focused inward rather than outward, is that the man who robbed you last week is walking past you. The information from your senses goes into your mind. Although the conscious mind is occupied, the subconscious mind still has the thought, "That looks like the man who robbed me." Since subconscious thoughts are below our level of awareness we do not know the thought took place. However, the trigger is still set off by that part of our mind. So you find yourself walking down the street thinking about bread, milk and cleaners when suddenly your heart rate and body temperature start increasing, you begin to feel anxiety and panic, and feel the urge to flee. You look around puzzled as to what is going on and why you are feeling the way you do, but you do not see him because he has already walked past you. What is also interesting is that it wouldn't matter whether or not it was the robber or someone that just looked like him. If there is enough resemblance to the original incident the trigger goes off and you experience the associated WEBSATs. In essence, the specific experience can become generalized to countless situations.

I believe that we have triggers going off around us all the time. Some of the triggers we may be aware of, but many we are not. This is why we experience many of the WEBSATs that we do.

Have you ever had an experience within seconds of meeting someone that you find yourself thinking, "I don't know what it is about him, but I don't like him?" Unbeknownst to you, it may be that he wears a shirt similar to the shirt your grandfather wore. Since your memory of your grandfather is that he always mistreated you, and this person subconsciously reminds you of your grandfather, you feel dislike toward him even though you really know nothing about this new person. Your perception of this new person is not pure. It is distorted by events from your past. It is a preconception. Psychologists might call this transference. Transference in therapy refers to unknowingly transferring the past onto the present.

Anything about a new person that you meet has the potential to trigger a reaction. It may be that his hairstyle subconsciously reminds you of a seventh grade teacher with whom you did not get along. Facial mannerisms may remind you of your first boss who fired you when you were growing up. His tone of voice may remind you of your next door neighbor who always picked on you. Something about this new person triggers a memory and whatever you feel towards that person in the memory you now begin to feel towards the new person. Sometimes these associations and triggers occur subconsciously, and other times they may occur consciously, such as, "Doesn't his laugh remind you of Uncle Bob's." This would be an example of a conscious trigger.

In a similar vein we have all met someone and within seconds felt comfortable with them, and found ourselves thinking, "I like her." How do we make such a quick decision? Some of the instances may be accounted for by the fact that she reminds us of someone from our past. Maybe the dress she's wearing reminds you of your third grade school teacher, who thought you were special. You felt affinity towards her, so now you have a similar good feeling towards this new woman. Perhaps her perfume reminds you of your Aunt Helen who always bought you an ice cream cone when you were a child. Maybe her petite size reminds you of your older sister who always seemed to adore you. Again, any characteristics of this woman you just met could remind you of someone from your past.

If this pattern of triggers and associations accounts for some of the feelings, thoughts and impressions we get in new situations we would also expect, therefore, to sometimes be wrong in those interpretations of new people. We may possibly find out later that the feelings or attitudes we had toward the new person were completely inaccurate or inappropriate since they were not really based on the new person. We would discover, for example, that the man we did not like at first, turns out to be a very nice person as we get to know him. It was as if we initially overlaid or superimposed on him an image or impression of who we thought he was, and now we just peeled off the overlay and can see the real him without distortion.

I believe that we all walk through this world with triggers frequently going off. The triggers or flashbacks are not just set off by people. It can be anything with which an association can be experienced. It can, for example, be objects, animals, places and times that activate the memory on a conscious level, an unconscious level, or both.

It isn't all bad though. Sometimes it is helpful. For instance, if we burned ourselves on a stove at age seven, then at age eight it benefited us when we felt some heat when we were too close to a stove. It made us cautious about putting our hand any closer. It became a pro-survival response. However, it becomes ineffective and contra-survival when it causes us to see situations in a distorted way. When this occurs we are not in present time. Part of us is living in the past. If a lot of these triggers and associations are frequently occurring for an individual, then very little of the person is in present time. Those individuals that it happens to a lot may find people often saying they are preoccupied, spacey, out of it, not quite there, detached or refer to them as an airhead.

Consider that I'm seven years old and I'm going excessively fast down a steep hill on my bicycle. Suddenly, I hit a small stone and the bike is out of control. I go flying off the bike hitting the ground. I end up with, among other things, a headache, disorientation, dizziness, and a need for 21 stitches. If we call this incident "Headache and Disorientation Related To a Bicycle" and if it is not already a book title in our library then this incident would become page one in that book.

Then at the age of fourteen, I am in a bike race and I collide with another cyclist. We fall to the ground and sustain some minor cuts and scrapes. I may consciously have the thought that this reminds me of when

I was seven years old and fell on my bike. At any rate, the trigger goes off, the switch gets thrown and I begin experiencing dizziness and a headache. This incident becomes page two in our book titled, "Headache and Disorientation Related to A Bicycle."

Then I'm 25 years old. My wife and I are at an outdoor display of bicycles and are looking at a bike for our eight year-old child. Without me realizing why, I start to feel dizzy and have a headache beginning. My wife asks me what is wrong. I tell her I have a headache and feel disoriented. Being human, we often attempt to understand what is happening to us, but we frequently mislabel it. In this instance my wife suggests that since it is quite hot outside today that maybe it's the heat causing it. She recommends we get inside an air-conditioned place and maybe I will feel better. We get into the car, unknowingly moving away from the triggering stimulus (the bike), turn the air on and fifteen minutes later I'm feeling better. We agree, "Yes, it must have been the heat." We have mislabeled the cause.

Another scenario might be that when I tell her that I have a headache and disorientation she asks if I ate breakfast before leaving the house. I tell her no and she suggests that if I get a bite to eat I might feel better. We go for lunch (unknowingly moving away from the triggering stimulus) and fifteen minutes later I'm feeling somewhat better. My wife shakes her finger at me, playfully chiding me that, "You've got to take time to eat breakfast in the morning." Again we mislabeled it. Even though we were not conscious of the trigger going off, it still occurred on a subconscious level. I was then pulled into the past picking up any or all of the WEBSATs in the original page one and page two situations and I begin re-experiencing it. This third incident, of course, becomes page three in the book, "Headache and Disorientation Related to A Bicycle."

As I have said, these events do not all have to be negative or traumatic. When explaining about how events from the past can affect us in the present I will often ask clients to recall a time when they told or heard a funny joke or experienced a situation that they thought was hilarious. Once they tap into the memory they will invariably begin smiling and/or laughing, since that emotion was contained in that earlier memory. I then explain that just as they went back in time in response to my request and touched on the memory, thus triggering a response in present time, that the same occurs with negative WEBSATs. We touch on a memory and we can re-experience anything that is in that memory.

I would like you to pause for a moment and think about a lemon. Try and have this visual image be as real as possible. You may be picturing the yellow color and the little pitted depressions all over it. See how the light reflects off the lemon and gives it a bit of a shiny appearance. Feel the smoothness of the skin. Now peel the lemon open. Put it up to your nose and smell it. Experience it. As you do, the tart smell gets even stronger in your nostrils. You encounter that intense, pungent, citric odor. Now bite into it. Again experience that tartness. Suck on the lemon and taste the juice that has that somewhat sour flavor. Feel how the tartness makes your mouth pucker as it touches your lips, tongue and mouth. Notice how it begins to make you salivate and swallow.

If you followed the directions above you probably had a physiological reaction to the image. You and your body reacted to an image as if it was the real thing. You were having a reaction based on an experience or group of related experiences from your past. You may have consciously recognized in this exercise that you tapped into memories from the past or it may have been completely unconscious. This is how we touch on some specific or general image or memory from the past and re-experience it in the present time.

I will explain methods later on how to reduce or eliminate the power that these past events have over us. To sum it up as concisely as possible at this point, I would recommend that you **be here now**. To "be" means to exist. "Here" means in this place and "now" means to be in present time. Keep actively working to keep yourself in present time. **Live consciously**. Diligently work at operating from a conscious state of mind. **Learn from the past, plan for the future, but live in the present.**

Experiencing the Cumulative Build-up

While explaining these theories to my patients in their therapy sessions I will ask them to do some role-playing. I ask them to play the role of Person A and later the role of Person B. I ask the patient to cross their legs and extend a leg out towards my feet. I then adjust my legs and "accidentally" lightly kick the foot of Person A who is attending their first session. I then say, "Oh, sorry." I continue talking a few minutes, rambling about something insignificant, and "accidentally" lightly kick their foot again and then apologize. I do this two or three more times. Then I ask how they think the average person would react if somebody was doing that to them. I tell them I would expect that the first time I accidentally kicked them, they might respond with a, "Oh, that's all right." The second time they might respond with, "Oh, no problem." The third time they may begin to feel a little annoyance or irritation. The fourth time they are actually annoyed and frustrated or they move their feet further away and out of the range of my "uncontrolled" feet. The fifth time they may actually be upset or angry and decide to leave the session. This might be the way a typical person might act.

Then I give them a little background history of Person B whom I am seeing for her first session. I tell them that Person B has a history of physical abuse, of which I am unaware. She was first hit by her father as a young child and was frequently hit by him for many years after that. Sprinkled in between those incidents she was also physically abused by her grandfather and her older sister. As a teenager she was also abused by her first and second boyfriends and later on by her husband.

I then tell the actual patient I'm seeing in the session that Person A may have acted in a fairly normal way with fairly normal responses to being accidentally being kicked in the foot. Person B, however, when tapped in the foot by my foot immediately goes into a rage yelling, "How dare you. I don't take that from anybody." She then storms out of my office. I tell my actual patient that I sit there looking perplexed as to why person B left, wondering what the heck that was all about. All I did was accidentally kick her foot and she responded as if I was half killing her.

What the difference is between Person A and Person B is their past history. Person A has no history of physical abuse, but Person B has a book titled "Physical Abuse" that contains 187 pages (i.e., 187 separate incidents of abuse). What happens is a cumulative build-up of the emotions that are in the incidents are re-experienced and then expressed. In this case it was anger. Imagine if we could measure the anger of her first incident (page one) of physical abuse in inches. Let us assume that it might be five inches tall. We add to that the second incident (page two) of physical abuse that was not as intense and which might measure four inches of anger. The third incident gave us 6 more inches. Bringing the cumulative anger in just these first three incidents to fifteen. So when I kicked Person B with my foot she wasn't really seeing me. In her mind (most likely her subconscious mind) she was seeing her father, her grandfather, her older sister, her two boyfriends and her husband. When I accidentally kicked her, my "crime" should have been punished with, at most, a one-inch high "fine", but she hit me with 1,142 inches of explosive anger. Pretty unfair isn't it? Well, not only do people do things like that to us, we do things like that to people.

While it is relatively easy to find incidents of people who have treated you that way, it is typically much more difficult to spot when you have done it to others. The two main reasons it is hard for us to recognize when we do it are because of our own denial (there's that nasty old ego again) or our unawareness. To increase our awareness we need to ask ourselves this: "Who's masks do I put on some people's faces?" In other words, try to find those situations where we project other people onto the person in front of us.

Time Shifts and Indicators of Present Time Detachment

Each time a trigger goes off we are pulled out of present time, and we have triggers going off around us frequently. One of the things that occur when a trigger goes off is that we go unconscious on some level. By unconscious, I do not mean a fainting, passing out or falling to the floor. What I am talking about is more of a fogginess or a fading of our present-time focus. It is losing some amount of our present-time consciousness or awareness. When a trigger goes off we lose consciousness to varying degrees, primarily based on whether unconsciousness is actually contained in the past event. **Every time a trigger goes off it creates some degree of unconsciousness.** Inherent in the simple act of a trigger going off, is being pulled into the past and therefore, out of present time, resulting in an experience of consciousness loss. The amount of unconsciousness that occurs can be substantial if any of the incidents that we go back to actually contain unconsciousness in them and probably most incidents contain some amount of unconsciousness. The unconsciousness is like a full or partial systems shutdown. A past incident that contains extreme trauma may leave us in present time with practically no awareness or consciousness at all. It could be a brief loss or one that lasts for a sustained period.

With triggers going off around us as we walk our way through life, how do we know when we are reliving the past or when we are actually in present time? The more subtle the trigger is and the less impact a trigger has on us in present time, the harder it is to detect when it goes off. There are, however, several factors I have discovered and have determined can help us to recognize when we are not, or someone else is not, in the moment, but rather reliving the past. Keep in mind that these are just general rules of thumb and I will explain some of the exceptions later.

Here are **five factors that can help you detect when you are out of present time.**

The first of these *Trigger Factors* is that **a shift or change occurs**. It can be a shift in sensation, emotion, behavior, thought and/or attitude. It seems that we tend to most often notice it as a change in mood. It also is very important to point out that it usually contains some amount of unconsciousness. You may, or may not, feel as if something comes over you.

Second, often **it comes out-of-the-blue**. Many times there seems to be nothing in present time to account for the change. You might feel depressed for instance, but when asked what is depressing you, there is nothing you can put your finger on. There is often no apparent explanation. This out-of-nowhere factor occurs when subconscious triggers go off.

Third is **the intensity of the response**. Certainly, a response can run the whole range from subtle and almost imperceptible to intense and explosive. However, the ones that typically tend to do the most damage are those which are intense and extreme. It wouldn't be feeling sad, but rather it would be a deep depression. It wouldn't be a slight annoyance; it would be an explosive rage. Nevertheless, we should keep in mind that even feeling just a little bit sad or slightly annoyed can be a result of triggers.

Fourth, **the shift occurs quickly**. It is typically fast. There is no step-by-step progression, as what happened to my client, "Person A", when she was accidentally kicked by me. When the trigger sets off a past experience or history, the person can go off like a skyrocket, such as when I accidentally kicked "Person B." There was no incremental scale of increased emotions (i.e., annoyance, irritation, aggravation, anger, and rage). She went from zero to ninety in three seconds. I have discovered that when I hear a particular word used to describe the behavior of a person, that the person being spoken about was not in present time. That word is ballistic. "You should have seen him. He went ballistic." Whenever you hear the word used, it is a safe bet to assume that whatever it is that triggers the reaction of "ballistic" for the person, there is a considerable likelihood of them having a past history issue which impacts greatly on them in present time.

Fifth is that usually **a response is disproportionate.** By this I mean that the punishment is much greater than the crime. I accidentally kick a person's foot and they storm out of the room. Another scenario is a husband who rarely has a drink, stops for a drink with his coworkers to celebrate a worker's birthday. He calls his wife to let her know what he is planning. She gets angry and yells and screams at him. Why such a disproportionate reaction? Her first husband was an alcoholic who spent all his time and money in bars. Her history may also include an alcoholic parent.

In general, although it may be difficult for a person to spot on their own, a close examination of the triggered incident will usually reveal illogical reasoning. A person may explode and create a World War III incident, for example, out of the fact that someone did not save him a piece of pizza.

The mind operates as a reactive unit. That is, the mind functions in such a way that when an event occurs in the present time it searches through the memory banks for a similar event or item. It then tells us how we reacted to that in the past. Next, and too often, we react to the present time event in the same way. This patterning of our behaviors hampers our learning and growing and locks us in to a more rigid world. When we are operating *from* the mind we are running our life on automatic. We are not fully being in each moment. We are not fully being in present time. What we need to do is release or detach ourselves to some extent from the control of the reactive unit that we call our mind. The mind confuses the present with the past. To begin to take back control, remember: **Now is not then.**

The mind, however, can also be a very helpful and effective tool. When we are getting dressed in the morning we do not have to put 100% of our attention on tying our shoes. That enables us to do more than one task at a time. At one point in time we were a child just learning how to tie a shoe. At that time we needed to give it 100% of our attention in order to be successful at shoe tying. After numerous successes at shoe tying we mastered the task. When we have learned and mastered all there is to learn about something, then we tend to put it on automatic. We then free ourselves up to do other tasks such as talk with someone, or watch TV while we tie our shoes. The mind is also great for analyzing and categorizing. Nevertheless, remember that the analytical process itself can be influenced and distorted by triggers, past history and defense mechanisms.

Unfortunately, too often we apply these automatic reactions to either events or items that we have not fully mastered or ones in which more learning is possible. For instance, look at automobile driving by teenagers. First, the accident rate is much higher for male teens. Second, I recently read in the newspaper that the death rate for sixteen year-old drivers in the U.S. is higher than any other age group of drivers. I believe this is because the teens feel that they have fully mastered the operation of a motor vehicle when in actuality they have not.

I believe we also put people on automatic. We think, for example, that we have learned all there is to learn about our spouse or partner. These unknown factors may account for the high divorce rate and the growing apart that occurs in relationships and marriages. Further, this can sometimes result in having known someone for a long time, only to find that you are really strangers. Whether it is items, events, or people, if we have not fully learned all there is to learn about it or them, then we are robbing ourselves. We are robbing ourselves of intelligence, awareness, wisdom and life. This is primarily because everything in this universe is in a constant state of change…a continuous state of flux. The way it was yesterday or even a minute ago is not necessarily the way it is now. Again this emphasizes the importance to Be Here Now.

Locating and Understanding the Pattern and Source of the Triggers

How do we go about recognizing and stopping the unwanted triggers from going off and reducing or alleviating the negative fallout when they do go off? First, it is essential to realize that thoughts, behaviors, emotions and attitudes do not change on their own. Picture a cue ball sitting in the middle of a pool table. How long do you suppose we would have to sit there and watch it until it moved on it's own. It wouldn't. Something has to move it. A pool stick, another ball, or some other outside force like an earthquake, a strong wind or someone bumping the table. Similarly, our thoughts, behaviors, emotions and attitudes do not change on their own. Something has to change them. So, if we are in a good mood and suddenly we feel sad we know that something had to cause it. Let us try something. If I say to you, "Be angry. Not *act* angry, but *be* angry." Or if I said, "Be ecstatic. Actually *be* ecstatic." You would likely say to me, "Well, I can't just be ecstatic or just be angry." "Why not?" "Well, because something has to happen first to make me feel that way." That is exactly right! Consequently, we cannot or do not feel an emotion, for example, without something first occurring, whether it is something in present time or something from the past, such as a trigger going off. It is the same whether something occurs internally, like a thought, or externally, such as something in our environment.

How do we determine what the cause of our mood shift was? Well, we know that the cause has to come before the effect. Therefore, if we ask ourselves **when did it begin and what took place just prior to that** we will begin to focus on the cause.

Let's say that I notice I'm feeling sad. I first look in present time to see if there is a present time explanation for the *amount* of emotion that I am experiencing. If my dog didn't die, my house didn't burn down, I didn't lose my job, my best friend didn't move away, etc. then I can likely eliminate a present time cause. If something did happen in present time, but it's not proportionate to the amount or intensity of the response, then it is probably related to past history. In other words, if the present time causal event was small and my emotional response or effect was intense, then it is most likely related to some past experience.

Once I have determined that there was no present time event to explain the amount of emotion I am feeling, I ask myself when did it begin ("Oh, about fifteen minutes ago") and what took place just prior to that? I then do an external and internal assessment. I try to determine what was in my external environment such as sitting on a couch, eating a sandwich, and watching the news on TV with my feet propped up on the coffee table. I assess everything in the external environment. Every color, shape, object, sound, movement, etc. While this may sound lengthy, it is amazing how quickly you can do this with practice. I then do an internal assessment. What was I thinking about just prior to the sadness? I was thinking that I was hungry and the sandwich tasted good (could have used more mayo), that I had to remember to give Steve a call, that the house fire they were showing on the TV news looked like a real bad fire, etc.

Following the assessments one of two things may happen. One, I may consciously locate the cause, such as that the fire reminded me of when I was four years old and started a fire in our home and we lost everything in the fire. Two, I might not consciously locate the cause. In this case I will just take all the information I have gathered, make note of it and put it away for now. When the next trigger goes off in my life I will do a similar assessment. Eventually patterns begin to show up such as, "Hey, isn't that interesting. It seems that when I read or hear about a house fire I get a sick feeling in my stomach and then I begin to feel sad."

Certainly, the sooner you can spot that a trigger went off, the easier it is to do the assessment. It is more difficult to remember what happened internally and externally three days ago than an hour ago. It is also more difficult to remember an hour ago than five minutes ago. Similarly, the more that you are in present time the easier it is to spot when a change occurs.

At times people experience waking up in the morning with a change in their mood from what it was when they went to bed. This could mean that they had a dream that resulted in the mood change or that a trigger went off during the dream.

Once you have found what the trigger appears to be and what your response to the trigger is (for example, feeling sadness about house fires) you can then begin to process it. There are two ways to use the information you have gained from the assessment on the trigger. One, is that you can *track the occurrences of the trigger* in your life looking for the earliest ones that occurred. These earliest episodes tend to be the root of that particular trigger and finding the earliest ones serves best to free you from their control. The second way is to *follow the reaction or response* you had when the trigger went off. Just relax and get in touch with the response. Re-experience it. Go back in time to your earliest memories of having that similar response. So, what you are doing with the first method is following the trigger or stimulus and looking for the books in our mind's library with titles relating to, for example, fires, house fires and dangerous situations. You could also use the second method and examine the books having "sick feeling in the stomach" or "sadness" in the title. This would be tracking the reaction or response.

As you find each individual incident (a page in the book), it is important to particularly explore and *feel* the emotions in them. *Re-experience* the emotions in each situation. This process is very critical because it drains the emotion and controlling power out of the past events. It takes the emotionally-laden events and diminishes or eliminates the cumulative build-up of emotion. It reduces the disproportionate and undeserved reactions to people, things and events in your present life. In other words, you will be more in present time and won't be pulled into the past. You will be seeing the present-time person, item or situation more clearly and more accurately. You will be seeing it as it is, rather than as a distorted image like in a fun house mirror. Some people might think that they will be giving up who they are. This is really not the case. In actuality it allows us to become more ourselves.

One way to picture this change in control occurring is by a series of boxes side-by-side becoming consecutively smaller. If you begin taking control of a trigger or habit you will notice three factors. These are *intensity, duration and frequency*. Let's imagine that you have a habit of cigarette smoking and you decide to take control of it and quit completely right now. Very quickly after finishing your last cigarette you may feel an almost instant urge to smoke again. The urge is quite strong (intensity) and can last a fairly lengthy time (duration). But then you do something, or something occurs which distracts you, and the urge briefly goes away before returning (frequency). So picture the intensity as the height of the box, the duration as the length of the box and the frequency as the gap between the boxes. The urge occurs again fairly quickly and begins a second box, but as you begin to take control you will notice that the trigger or habit begins to lose power. Hence, the next urge or trigger (the next box) is not quite as intense (height) and does not last quite as long (length). As this process continues the frequency with which the trigger or habit occurs is less. So what we generally have with this Box Reduction Pattern is a series of side-by-side boxes that over time continue to reduce in size with the gaps between the boxes getting longer.

In what other ways does the mind with it's triggers negatively impact on our lives? As author Marianne Williamson pointed out in material from "A Course In Miracles", the genuine experience of something disappears when we mistake our mental images and past memories for the experience itself. It is similar to the difference of eating a chocolate bar and watching someone on TV eat a chocolate bar. It is like the distinction between swimming in the ocean and imagining swimming in the ocean. The TV and the images are not the real experience of what swimming and chocolate are. If we see the context of something, such as mental images, and misidentify them as the content (i.e., the actual experience) we lose whatever the actual experiences would have been. We become so focused on the *context* of the chocolate bar with such judgments as: will it make me fat; is it too close to dinner time; should I have spent the money; am I addicted to chocolate; and so on that we lose sight of the *content* of the experience. That is, the genuine experience of eating and enjoying the chocolate bar itself. Similarly, *saying* the word chocolate is not the same as *eating* chocolate. You can describe chocolate with a variety of descriptive words, but it still is not the same as actually tasting it. In some cases confusing the content for the context can be devastating. For example, while making a speech in front of 200 of our peers we misspeak and flub some lines. We then become so focused on whether we will be perceived as a poor speaker, a stupid person, or that they may no longer want to be associated with us that we completely freeze up and cannot continue with the speech.

So what would happen if we were to not get caught up in the context and if we were to remove all our triggers, fears and negative emotions? We would be fully in the moment and we would begin to experience the pure essence of a human being. We would see all other beings and things without distortion. We would see in each being what is in the center of all beings. **The true nature and core of all beings is goodness.** Recognizing the truth in this statement would bring understanding and compassion.

Distortions Created by the False Self

Two of the obstacles to achieving this goal are the parts of the mind we call the ego and the id. They have needs and they want to get their needs met. The ego is like our perceived self and the id is more like a spoiled child. The id wants what it wants, and it usually wants it now. If it does not get what it wants it throws a tantrum and makes your life miserable. It constantly nags you for what it wants. It typically demands immediate gratification. Even when the obsessive or addictive needs of the id and ego are met it only reinforces them. They may be temporarily subdued, but a short time later they are looking to get their needs met again. Often there is a pattern of id and ego wanting an increasing amount of whatever it is. This is a sure sign that that they will never be satisfied, no matter how much they get. The only way to end this cycle is to stop feeding them.

Some of the fuels that help to power the ego are negativity, over-reaction, resistance and fear. These fuels are based on the mind's experience of our past. The ego, therefore, feels that it must keep the past activated in order to keep our present self alive since the ego believes our past determines who we are in the present, and concludes that we would be nothing without it. Not only does this process create a *false self*, but the whole concept and belief is totally false. It actually leads us astray and keeps us from re-discovering our true self as a spiritual being. When the mind and ego are not busy keeping us blindly living in the past, they are joining forces to keep our attention focused on the future. They do this by thrusting an image of our false self into the future and predicting for us that when we arrive there everything will be wonderful. They tell us that we will get that big house, drive that great car, have those fancy clothes, possess that huge bank account, obtain that fabulous job or whatever it is that we have in our future prediction that is supposed to bring us happiness, status and prestige. The problem with all this is that by buying into this distortion (our false self) we become past and future-focused and are never allowed to be in the present where we encounter and experience our true self. The mind and ego keep us out of "the now" by telling us that the present is unimportant, and that the present is no more than a stepping stone to what is paramount. It wants us to believe that the destination is more important than the journey and that the past and future have more merit than the present.

One of the problems with the false self is that it gives us an external concept of who we are. Which couldn't be further from the truth. It is as if we are seeing our self through the eyes of others. We are led to believe that who we are is based on our finances, career (or lack thereof), possessions, physical appearance, social status, achievements, and our blunders and mistakes.

Understanding life and who we are begins with our getting the biggest picture of life that we can. It is attempting to see beyond the limitations of our physical eyes. Some people may say that as spiritual beings we have existed since the beginning of time. Since time is only relative to the physical world and does not exist on the spiritual plane it suggests that we existed *before* the beginning of time. That being the case, it seems likely that we have lived a multitude of past lives. And in those lives we have been old and young, rich and poor, weak and strong, vicious and kind, male and female. Our skin color has likely been black, white, brown, yellow and red. At one time or another we may have belonged to every religion, culture, social standing, and age group that exists. Or that ever existed.

It is interesting how Shakespeare's famous quote fits in so well with the concept of past lives. He said, "All the world's a stage, and all the men and women merely players; they have their exits and entrances, and one man in his time plays many parts." Given how long we may have existed we could feasibly have played every role that there is to play on these stages.

It is important to understand the concept of roles because of how easily roles can trap us. If we were to ask someone who they think they are we could get a variety of responses. These may include father, brother, friend, neighbor, painter, sports fan and so on. These are not, however, who we are. These are just roles we are playing. When we play these roles we usually wear the appropriate costumes and have the necessary props to play the part. When we take these roles to be *who we are,* rather than recognize that we are spiritual beings, the roles just become another part of the false self. We should not confuse the roles we are playing in this lifetime, with who we actually are. We are not what we do, what we have or what others think of us. I see the false self as being made up of two components that are closely connected. One, if we allow them to, are the roles that we take on. The second is more of a character structure of the mind. It is a perceived self or an assumed identity. It is as if we take on an alias. This alias, or false self, uses defense mechanisms (described later in the book) to supposedly protect us from believed harm. It urges and drives us to think, speak and act based on painful events from the past, or perceived threats in the present or future. This false self forms distorted and over-reactive perceptions, beliefs and theories about how life *is*. And then tells us what character traits, and attitudes we supposedly need to maintain in order to survive.

The Path of Love

When we ponder Shakespeare's quote and the playing of roles it seems to beg the question of what the purpose is to all these lives. I believe the common denominator in all life is the pursuit of growth. We are here to grow, to learn and to remember. The reasons I say 'to remember' are because we have forgotten that we are spiritual beings, that we have a long and rich history stored in our subconscious and spiritual library, and we have lost conscious awareness of the source from which we came.
Basically, I see our life purpose as being two-fold. One is to achieve personal growth and the second is to serve others. It's interesting to note that an increase in one tends to then bring about an increase in the other. I believe that the greatest goal of life is to have a positive effect. We get to choose our goals and the path we take. **The path that leads to the fastest and greatest growth is the path of love.**

One may say that some people are not growing. Take for example, a murderer. It would seem obvious that they are not growing towards love and awareness. I believe, however, that they are. It is similar to how it might take centuries for a constant dripping of water to finally wear through a rock. I clearly do not condone the actions of a murderer, and, in fact, I disagree entirely with that as a solution to the issues that they are working their way through. There are more effective and less damaging approaches to use. I do, however, believe that they are on a path of growth. We tend to not see it because we are looking at their life from too narrow a perspective and therefore, see no growth. We need to enlarge our view and see it across all their lifetimes. It would be similar to looking at a salesman's weekly sales and conclude that he is not growing as a salesman because there was no improvement in sales from last week to this week. If, however, we compared his sales from one year ago to now we observe a significant positive improvement. The murderer has just not gotten as far along the road of growth and awareness as many others have. Each and every one of us is someplace on this road. Some are farther up the road than we are and some are farther back down the road. The murderer may not make his change today or even tomorrow. At present he sees murder as his best option and he may not grow beyond murdering until his next lifetime, but he is moving toward God. Just as day always follows night, every step that darkness takes is one step closer to the light. The lives of all beings contain one identical and unavoidable premise. **All roads lead to God.** It is just that some roads are more dangerous and treacherous. Some take longer and others may initially take you out of your way or even in the wrong direction. Some people are moving forward, but have not yet figured out their best personal route for getting them where they want to go. Others, like the murderer, wander aimlessly because they may not even realize that they are on the road of spiritual evolution. They are oblivious to the fact that they are on a road at all and that the road actually leads somewhere.

Answers Provided by Past Lives

The concept of past lives offers possible answers to numerous questions and explanations for puzzling phenomena. For instance, it would explain geniuses that have existed at various times in our human history. Mozart was said to have composed incredibly complex music at the age of four. Many people find this incomprehensible. However, if Mozart had been a musician or composer in the past life, or several past lives, just prior to his years as Mozart it would help to explain it. The mind stores records of all the information from all our senses. If past lives exist, the mind would store all the information from all our senses from all our lifetimes. This information about music composition would, therefore, be stored in Mozart's mind. It appears that most of the information from our present lifetime gets stored in the conscious mind. The information from our past lives is stored in our subconscious mind when we are born into our next new lifetime. Mozart may have been far enough up the road of awareness to where he could more readily access some of his past talent and knowledge about music. Another possibility is that as he interacted with music materials in his Mozart lifetime that it triggered memories (or some form of subconscious leakage) from a past life that he was able to use in his Mozart lifetime. Similarly, it may be the same for most or all geniuses. Those that some people call idiot savants may be accessing information from past lives, tapping in to their super-conscious mind, or the UniverSOUL library at level five.

Mozart's age may have also played a factor. The younger we are the easier it may be to access memories from past lives. Possibly much of what we call the vivid imagination of young children may be related to prior past lives. One may look at the book "Audrey Rose." It is about a small child who, to the astonishment of her parents, is apparently able to access her prior past life.

It has been said that humans only use a small percentage of their brains. Is this because much of the brain is used to handle and control the storage of information of all the lifetimes from our past?

It may be that when we align ourselves, with jobs or interests in this lifetime with learnings from the past lives, that there is a natural inclination to be drawn to it, to learn it easier and to be more effective at the task, job or service. We often hear the phrase; "It just seems to come naturally to him."

In some cases it may explain obsessions and compulsions. Impulses, images, thoughts or ideas that are repetitive and persistent, seem involuntarily produced and appear to invade our conscious mind are called obsessions. Compulsions are defined as behaviors that are repetitive and seem to be driven by an irresistible inner force compelling a person to perform the action even though it may be against their own "will." The compulsions typically involve certain rules or rituals and the performance of the act does not bring pleasure, but rather seems to bring some relief of tension.

Individuals may have a drive or urge to gamble based on a past life as a gambler. Another person might have an obsession and/or compulsion about orderliness. Possibly in a past life they experienced some life trauma when they were not orderly. As a way to avoid present and future trauma (or the tension related to the trauma) they become obsessive/compulsive about it. It may be that in a past life the person created a belief system or formed an intention around the idea that a lack of orderliness led to negative consequences and therefore, they now operate on that belief or intention in present time.

Similarly, a soldier who died on a battlefield during the War Between the States may not have died immediately, but breathed in goldenrod pollen for hours while dying. The pollen now becomes, in his mind, associated with death. In a following lifetime or lifetimes he may experience what we call an allergic reaction to that pollen. Or possibly he develops asthma in this lifetime because of his difficulty breathing in the previous lifetime as a result of the pollen. Another example is that a person who has a fear of water in this lifetime may have drowned or had a near-drowning in a previous life.

This does not mean that there cannot be other reasons for asthma, allergies, sensitivities, child geniuses, obsessive/compulsive disorders, chronic depression, addictions, anxiety, fears and so on. There certainly could be other causes or explanations, but what the percentages are of past lifetime causes versus other causes is presently unknown.

In the field of psychology we often search for a traumatic event that a person experienced in their earlier years (in this lifetime) as a reason why they now have, for example, a fear of water. At times we are unable to find anything that accounts for it. It just seems to make sense that if a person has a fear of water now, then he may have had a bad or traumatic experience with water at an earlier time. Typically, when we are unable to find something in this lifetime to account for the fear, we assume that either there is no past event or that a person just cannot remember it. If we can accept the theory that fears and phobias are caused by past traumas, then it is not that much of a stretch of logic to consider that if the event is not found in this lifetime then it could be that the cause or source came from an even earlier time. So, the problem may be that we are just not looking back far enough in time. In a sense, it may be that it is like looking at one page in a book and trying to determine what the book is about rather than knowing what is on every page.

Past life traumas may account for transvestism. Transvestism is the desire to, and/or the act of wearing clothes of the opposite gender, but having uncomfortable feelings when dressed in the clothing of one's own gender. Could it be plausible that a man may wish to dress as a woman due to the fact of having been a woman in a previous life and where the experience in that life was one of love and happiness, but the lifetime was cut short by their death. The present lifetime may or may not be a happy one, but in the recesses of the mind the man has memories of a wonderful life as a woman and feels an urge to get that happiness back. This he may attempt to achieve by dressing as a woman. It may likewise explain some of the transsexual cases. A transsexual is an individual with an overwhelming desire to become the opposite sex. Of course, this does not rule out the possibility that there may also be other explanations for these desires.

Certainly, all of our past lives history does not have to be traumas and dredging up negative and unhappy events. Past lives may explain why we have likes and dislikes, preferences, eccentricities, idiosyncrasies, and prejudices. It could explain affinities for particular languages, cultures, countries or cities. It may account for any favorite art, furniture, themes and motifs in our homes, such as French furniture or American southwest designs and furnishings. We may have a fondness for a particular time in history like the civil war, roaring twenties, wild west, medieval times or Egypt when the pharaohs ruled. We seem to just feel drawn to some things, people, places, events and times.

Past lives could explain birthmarks, warts, growths or scars on the body that are not due to something that occurred in this lifetime. Perhaps that was a place on your body in a previous lifetime that received some trauma by a knife, bullet or burn for example.

Think for a minute and try to imagine what some of the traumas could be that would create some of the fear responses that we have. Keep in mind that fears go far beyond just the physical, such as fear of water, snakes and rats. Fears could also be financial (fear of being poor), social (fear of being in large crowds), psychological (fear of small spaces, fear of heights) and emotional (fear of expressing anger). Some fears fall into several categories like the fear of failure.

Logically, any and all fears and phobias seem to come from past events in this or previous lifetimes. It may be the same for many pains, chronic headaches and impairments.

If we accept the theory of past lives, does it not offer a possible explanation for those religious experiences that are labeled “speaking in tongues”? Perhaps they are speaking a long lost language from a past life. If at the time they are experiencing a spiritual uplifting they may be operating for that brief period at a higher vibrational rate and at that level are able to access the memories from a previous lifetime. They may have tapped into their spiritual library system. Furthermore, every once in a while we will read about a case in the field of psychology where some individual experienced a head injury or a blow to the head. This person then began fluently speaking a language such as French that they had never learned or spoken in this lifetime.

There have been countless reports of out-of-body and near-death experiences. When this has occurred we invariably hear it described as looking down at, or over at the body. If we are actually bodies, then we would expect a person to be perceiving from the viewpoint of the body. If we are spiritual beings, then coming from a viewpoint outside of or around the body makes perfect sense. This may also account for reports of people experiencing a sense that someone is behind them even though nothing was heard or seen. Then they turn around and sure enough someone is standing there. It could be that since, as spirits, we extend beyond our bodies that we may have touched the other person's spirit, even though we did not physically touch them. It could be the same phenomena transpiring when we sense that someone is watching us. Just how far does the spirit extend? If I were a betting person I would say to infinity. This could offer an explanation for those situations where something traumatic or sudden happens to a loved one and we get a sense that something is wrong.

Past lives and their impact on our present lives may be a hidden or confounding variable in much research of the mind. It may be a factor that is not being considered in the equation when research is being done. Therefore, it could create misperceptions and not allow us to fully understand the true explanations for attitudes, behaviors, perceptions, thoughts and mental workings.

It seems a likely probability that most, if not all, of the aberrant behavior of humans may be due to traumas that occurred and decisions that were made in past lives. There are three forms in which these sources of disturbance may occur. A source may be from an incident in which something was done to us. It may be an incident in which we did something to someone or something. It could also be a situation where someone or something did something to another someone or something.

There are several final thoughts on the subject of past lives. One thought is the issue of déjà vu. Deja vu is defined as the illusion of having already experienced something that is actually being experienced for the first time. Is it possible that déjà vu is not an illusion, but is simply the experience of an event that is similar in some ways to an event from a past life? Those that have experienced it seem to say with certainty that they feel as if they have experienced it before even though they cannot seem to recall when. It may be some form of subconscious leakage or that the similarity of some aspect of the present time event triggered the memory from the past.

A second thought is that I expect that part of the coming world spiritual changes will be a recognition that past lives do exist, and that in the truest sense, death does not exist. I anticipate that with the help of others at first, we will be able to have contact with spiritual beings from our Earthly lives that have "died" and passed on. With time, I expect that we will all have the ability to be in contact with these spiritual beings on our own. This will bring about the end of the concept of death, as we now know it. In a sense, it will be the death of death. **Our lives will end where they began, beyond eternity and infinity.**

The final thought on this subject is that if the history and details of all of our past lives are stored in the subconscious mind then what would life be like if we could access it all. The enlightened spirit known as Plato over two thousand years ago had a word to describe this process. Plato used the word *anamnesis* to label the action of recalling previously experienced ideas of the soul that existed in another life. Presently we are trying to live our lives based on the experiences and knowledge we have gained in this lifetime. If we were able to access this past information and learn from it, then we would likely make fewer mistakes in present time or at least not make the same mistakes over and over again. As the philosopher George Santayana explained, **"Those who cannot remember the past are condemned to repeat it."**

Just imagine what it would be like if instead of basing our life on the information in one book (our present lifetime) we based it on all the knowledge and experience contained in our whole library. The goal is to remember the past, but not let it control us or prevent us from achieving awareness and growth. That was then, this is now. **Don't let the past infect the present.**

Awareness and Growth as a Two-Step Process

I visualize awareness and growth as a two-step process. First, we want to reduce the unwanted power and control of the mind and it's triggers. Also, we want to be very clear that we are not our mind. Second, we want to develop new and effective ways of taking back control of our lives in order to better understand life, express ourselves and interact in more loving ways with others.

How do we help break free of the hold our mind and our past has over us? One way to begin the process is to list and examine our primary beliefs. We need to look at our beliefs about our self. List our beliefs about others (other people, couples, families, cultures, races, religions, financial status, physical appearance, etc.). What are our beliefs about the world and how it is or how it isn't? Our beliefs about the future? Our beliefs about God or a supreme being? The degree of awareness gained from this process will be proportional to the degree of our willingness to be completely honest with ourselves.

Challenging Our Belief Systems

We can discover much about ourselves by looking at our beliefs. Many of our beliefs were handed to us by parents, teachers and clergy, but we have very likely never tested the accuracy of the beliefs. Even those beliefs that appear accurate may be inaccurate because of the fact that by simply holding a particular belief we may actually then create it in reality. For example, if I have a belief that I cannot win a particular game, then there is a good likelihood I will lose the game (a negative self-fulfilling prophecy). Similarly, if I believe that I catch colds easily, then I better be carrying tissues with me at all times. What is also so ironic and interesting about this is that the act of simply carrying the tissues reinforces or helps support the belief that I catch colds easily. Likewise, every time I catch a cold it "proves" to me that my belief is accurate. Wow, talk about a merry-go-round.

In other cases we may have had a very specific event occur which we later generalized to cover all, or nearly all, the cases of it. These generalizations are often called stereotypes. Suppose I get robbed and it happens to be by a 160-pound foreigner. I then may form a belief that all foreigners are out to rob people. That belief makes no more sense than a belief that all people who weigh 160 pounds are out to rob you.

We have probably all heard someone say, "Men can't be trusted." This belief may have come into existence because a woman once had a boyfriend who cheated on her or betrayed her in some way. Just because someone can give an instance of something happening does not make it true in every case. One board does not make a house. Yet we still choose to cling to many beliefs that we created this way.

Our beliefs have much power over us. To the extent that one believes one's happiness is only attainable through someone or something else – it becomes so. To the extent that one believes the problems in one's life are caused by someone else and are therefore, unsolvable – then they are.

A further problem is that we take our beliefs and tend to treat them as facts. It is more accurate and effective to recognize them as hypotheses when we are in the information gathering mode. When we do, we can then begin to test the hypothesis. Does it remain true in all cases all of the time? Don't let your belief get in the way of testing your belief. Be open-minded.

One way to test a belief, although it is certainly not foolproof, is to observe a third party in relation to the belief. For instance, does your coworker distrust all men all of the time? If not then you may need to examine the truthfulness of your own belief. Just keep in mind that this is not a perfect system either because she may hold the same belief system you do and therefore be creating the same reality. She may also have formed her belief based on one specific experience that she then generalized to all experiences. She may have gotten her belief from the same source (i.e., a teacher, parent, clergy, or the community). Also, just because a large number of people believe something to be true does not make it so. Once there was a common belief that the world was flat. It was assumed that the earth was the center of the universe and the sun revolved around the earth. A majority of German people once believed it was okay to kill millions of people because those people were believed to be of an inferior race. Americans carried out a similar action against the Native American.

Go observe a number of people if possible. Read books. Talk to other people. Get other people's views. Ask yourself if your belief could be based on skewed or distorted data or based on a fairly singular observation. Our beliefs can be divided into two categories; those that we have consciously chosen, and those that we have not. Those beliefs that we have not consciously chosen can be subdivided into three categories. They are those that were programmed into us, those that we blindly accepted without question and those that were forced upon us. In addition, we could have a belief that is based on another belief. If the primary belief is false then it is likely the secondary one is also. Challenge your beliefs. Start by making a list of a dozen or more. Take them one at a time and attack them from different points of view and see if they hold up. Do not try to prove them right. Try to disprove them. Release yourself from your old outdated and inaccurate beliefs. Do not fear this. If your beliefs are solid they will be able to withstand the scrutiny.

How powerful are our beliefs? Give some thought to this statement: **Life and reality are simply reflections of one's beliefs.** Our beliefs are what form the basis of our reality and our life. It is just that our misperception has brought about us not knowing which one creates which one. Let's be clear though. Your beliefs, which are manifested through your thoughts, communications, and actions, are what create your reality.

One of the most effective ways I have found for bringing about change in my own life has been the use of phrases. By phrases, I am referring, for example, to the quotes and sentences that you will find in the bold type in this book. The effectiveness seems to be a consequence of a number of factors. One is that phrases are brief and concise. A lot of knowledge or information can be compressed into a small space. Two, a phrase is easier to recall than a theory or a lengthy discourse. Three, in times of trauma, tension or situations that require a fast response they can be easily remembered and applied. Indeed, I have discovered that a simple phrase can change my life in a very profound way.

Again I emphasize that it is the *application* of these ideas, words and phrases that bring about change. The phrases need to be lived. I don't ask you to take my word for the truth in these phrases. Don't buy them…try them. Test them. Find what is true for you. If they work for you, aid you in improving your life, or help you to be more of who you are then make them yours.

Many years ago in my private psychological practice I thought about the process of creation. My explorations led me to believe that the process consisted of three steps. I came to see that the process began with a thought or an idea that we expressed in words. Then we put the thought or idea into action and created reality. I had been employing this procedure of thoughts, words and actions to help clients achieve their goals with good success for many years. Years later I read "Conversations with God" by Neale Donald Walsch and in his book he also described a three-step process that he called thought, words and deeds. Understanding this three-step process provides us with some powerful insights into our creative modus operandi.

The Power of Conscious Creation with Thoughts, Words and Actions

We create the world around us with our thoughts, words and actions. An easy way to remember this is to think of the airline TWA. I often notice that when a person begins to have some frustrating, resentful or angry thoughts that these thoughts often leak out or are expressed verbally, either by the choice of words or the tone of voice in their words, or both. These words often lead to angry actions. And as expected, we can usually count on getting a similar angry, frustrated or resentful response back from the world around us.

Why TWA? Because thoughts are in our mind. They are totally internal. Actions are totally external. Words are the precise steppingstone or gradient between the internal and the external. It takes something internal and makes it external. An internal thought is externalized into an action that creates a reality. In addition, words form inside our head and as we express them verbally we create a physical reaction by creating vibrations and moving particles through space. So, the expression of our thought by words truly does create a physical effect in the world.

You may ask, can a thought really create reality? Well, we have all had experiences of thinking of someone, the phone rings and it's them. Or we thought about getting some iced tea and someone yells from the kitchen and asks if we want some. Maybe you've thought about closing the window because it seemed chilly and someone else gets up to close it.

Since we are connected with God, there is little difference, at times, between our thoughts and prayers. We can not *see* thoughts or prayers, but while it may seem far-fetched, thoughts and prayers do have the power to create. I read a recent article about some surprised researchers at Columbia University. They conducted a study that found that women at an in vitro fertilization clinic in Korea had a higher pregnancy rate when complete strangers were praying for their success. These women, who were totally unaware of the praying, became pregnant twice as often as those women who were not being prayed for. The findings are in a current Journal of Reproductive Health.

All creation begins with a thought. **The smallest unit or building block of creation is a thought.** Whether it is building a piece of furniture, choosing a career, writing a poem or deciding what to have on the dinner menu. It all begins with a thought. The poet Ralph Waldo Emerson recognized the truth in this when he concluded that, "the ancestor of every action is a thought."

I can remember when I *thought* about and expressed the idea of becoming a psychologist (which set many of my friends howling). I followed up on the thought with written and spoken *words*. I talked to colleges. I read books and spoke with people in the field. I spoke to the bank and the school financial aide officer about finances. I filled out written applications at the bank and school. Next came more words (listening and speaking in class, reading and writing assignments) and the *action* of going to school. Finally I was given a degree that said I was a doctor in the field of psychology. It was now *reality.* Up until a certain time in my life the idea of being a psychologist was not even a thought. It is now a reality that I created. TWA is one of the most powerful tools we have as humans to create the reality in the world that we want. We can use the tool to create almost unimaginable joy. Unfortunately, we can also use the tool, consciously and subconsciously, to create the unhappiness that often exists in our lives.

You say, "Okay, I can understand using TWA to create wonderful things in my life, but what about the negative or bad things that happen to me. Why would they occur? Why would I create them? I don't want them in my life." They occur because on some level in our past or present we have created them. An example of a negative creation could be as subtle as a person thinking to himself (thought), "I probably won't be hired for the job." Then he tells his family (words) that he does not feel that he did well on the job interview. He then begins planning interviews for other jobs (action). He later finds out that he did not get the original job he wanted (reality). Very likely, he then uses this to "prove" that his feelings were accurate. It is the same process by which a positive thought, word or action in present time can create reality. For example, take something as simple as experiencing the thought, "My throat feels dry. I want something to drink." Then you either ask someone for a drink (words) or you go get a drink (action). Using a more complex example, you decide you no longer like where you work and you want a job elsewhere (thought). So you ask (spoken words) friends and business associates about job opportunities. You read through the want ads in the newspaper (written words). You put together and send out a resume (action with written words) and go to job interviews (action with spoken words). You eventually get hired (reality).

Knowing that our thoughts have the power to create, what do we do when we have negative or obsessive thoughts about something? First, having a thought does not mean we have to spend time focusing on that thought. A colleague suggests that we view our thoughts as cars going by. You can just be an observer and watch them go by. And just because one stops it does not mean you have to get in for a ride, especially if the driver seems to be of questionable character. You get to choose. You have that power. Why spend time with a negative or upsetting thought? Recognize also that this equally applies to our urges to say or do something.

Once you are in the car you can let the thought take you wherever it wants. Explore it if you choose to. You can also decide to drive the thought to where you want it to go. You can direct it. Of course, an excellent way to travel is getting into cars that are going to take you to where you want to go.

Do the cars you get into (thoughts, words and actions) take you to where you want to go? If not, why do you get in them? Why would you want to get into a car that takes you to someplace other than where you want to go? If you wish to become more conscious and more in control of your life, constantly ask yourself, "Does this take me in the direction that I say I want to go"?

If we are not having a thought, word or action in the present time that can account for the reality we are experiencing then it may be coming out of our past. Somewhere in the past we formed a belief. We may be aware of this belief or we may have forgotten it. At any rate, our subconscious mind has not forgotten it. We may, for example, have financial problems in present time. We cannot understand why it is happening because we want to get ahead financially. We work very hard to create financial well-being, but it just doesn't seem to happen. This is often because there is an underlying hidden belief in our past. Possibly throughout our upbringing our father was frequently saying, "We're common middle-class folks and people like us never get ahead." With that belief he creates that reality. As we are growing up we hear his words and see that reality, but we do not realize that he is creating it. Instead we believe that his words are obviously true because they match the reality. On some level we then agree with the belief and create the same reality for ourselves.

On the other hand suppose dad is a success, but he keeps telling us that we will never succeed like him and we will never amount to anything. If we experience several failures growing up, as we all do, but keep hearing his words, we may begin to think that he might be right. If we accept this as a belief we will then be building failure into our future. In a sense, our thoughts and actions for success in present time can be defeated by a stronger primary or *overriding thought* from the past. This can occur with our beliefs, intentions, thoughts, words or actions. We can have counter-beliefs, counter-intentions, counter-thoughts, counter-words and counter-actions buried in our past that are controlling our present and future and preventing us from attaining our present-time goals. We need to root out these negatives and rid ourselves of them. Our goals should be to increase the positive beliefs, intentions, thoughts, words and actions and reduce or alleviate the negative, contra-survival ones.

I imagine a balancing scale where all the weight and power lie on the negative side. In order to shift the balance the other way I need to put more weight on the opposite end, which is the positive side. I reduce the negatives by countering their power with weight or ammunition that I use on that opposite side. These are counter-beliefs (I believe that I'm meant to make a good financial living), counter-intentions (I'm going to do everything I can to be financially successful), counter-thoughts (I have plenty of money), counter-words (I am becoming more and more financially successful) and counter-actions (doing activities that increase the chances of my financial success). As the weight and power shift to the positive side we are then doing all we can to create the reality we want. When the counter-beliefs have overcome the earlier beliefs they then become our new beliefs. Any belief that goes against this new belief would then be classified as counter-beliefs.

Negative Self-fulfilling Prophecies and Dumping on Ourselves

The pattern of using our beliefs or expectations to set ourselves up for failure has long been known in psychology as a negative self-fulfilling prophecy. Perhaps I might see the boss walking past my office door with a cup of coffee in his hands. He looks in at me and gives what appears to be an annoyed look. I wonder why he is looking at me that way. I assume he is angry with me and that he is probably going to fire me. I become very upset by this because I have been working very hard for him. I think to myself that if he wants to treat me this way then to hell with him. I'm not going to break my back for him anymore. So I start slacking off on my work, coming in late and leaving early. Eventually, he calls me in to his office. He says that my work has become unsatisfactory and therefore, he is letting me go. I think, "See I was right. I knew he was going to fire me." What I did not know though was that he wasn't angry with me at all when he walked past my office. What happened was that just prior to passing by my office door he had taken a sip of his coffee. When he did he found that the milk in it was sour. This put a sour look on his face, which I took to be a scowl, at the same time that he just happened to be glancing in my office.

Had this actually happened in reality, I would have been the creator of this negative situation. I predicted I was going to get fired. I then fulfilled the prophecy myself with my beliefs, expectations, intentions, thoughts, words and actions. Hence, I created a negative self-fulfilling prophecy. As humans, we do this in our lives without ever realizing that we created the negative event. Every time we make a prediction or possess an explanation that is negative we are contributing energy toward bringing it into reality. Isn't it about time that we end these self-defeating creations?

If you are a person who just cannot accept the concept that we create all of the reality we experience then consider this alternative approach. Imagine you are driving out onto a street and have a green light. You no sooner get out into the intersection than another car runs a red light and hits you. You had the green light and the right of way. You could say that you did nothing wrong and that you did not create the accident. It was life dumping on you. Okay, let's say that. Let us also say that the actual accident lasted only two brief seconds. Are you able to just pretend that the accident did not happen and have it just go away? No, you can't. It's reality. It happened. But what you can choose is how you will handle and react to the situation. You could jump from your car yelling and screaming at the other driver. Maybe even hitting him or kicking his car while you are in a state of rage.

Do you like being in a state of rage? I don't. I would imagine most people don't. Do you like being angry? Hostile? Out of control? Most of us don't. One thing we can learn is that we have the ability to choose how we react to something. That does not mean that it comes under our control overnight. When we are in the midst of overreaction it is as if we are drunk on emotions. By releasing the painful emotions from our past and working on controlling our reactions in the present, it can be accomplished. I've been down that angry path enough times in my own life. **Do your best to not let the heat of the moment ignite your anger, because being closest to the source you will surely be the one to suffer the harshest injuries.**

I don't like that anger path because I know what waits for me down there. It's a dead-end street. It takes you nowhere. The only reward there is the booby prize. It not only does not help improve the situation, but it actually adds to the problem. Anger generates a lot more heat than it does light. Do not be a puppet to your anger. Just because you have a thought, it does not mean you have to act on it. Just because you have an emotion, it does not mean you have to be controlled by it.

So, imagine you are standing at a fork in the path. You know where the angry "Path A" would take you and you have chosen not to go there. Instead you choose to take "Path B". On "Path B" you get out of your car, check yourself over, realize you have no bodily injury and ask the other driver if he is okay. You find out he is okay and you exchange license and insurance information. Don't you much prefer this side of yourself?

Imagine that we take those two seconds (the length of time that the accident took) and represent it as the height of a nickel. Then we examine the emotions of the person who chose "Path A". Let us say that he was angry and frustrated about the accident for a full two weeks and displayed it by getting upset, cursing and being irritable. If we take the two seconds (a nickel) and calculate it for a two-week period we would get a stack of nickels that would be roughly equivalent to more than a 200-story building. This is equal to the Empire State Building being stacked on top of the Empire State Building. Now let us compare by placing one nickel on the sidewalk next to this building. The height of one nickel is equal to the actual length of time of the accident. The 200-story building is equal to how long you let the incident upset you. So, life dumped on you for the height of one nickel and you dumped on yourself for the height of a 200-story building. It is important to really understand just how extreme this difference is. Imagine standing on the sidewalk looking up at a building that is 200 stories tall.

We can stop blaming other people and other things for our moods and start taking personal responsibility for our emotions. We have the choice of turning the focus on ourselves or continuing to blame others for our self-inflicted wounds. One of the problems is that: **We tend to take credit for our successes, but blame others for our failures.** We want to perceive the source of our problems as being outside of ourselves. Our negative painful experiences however, are not caused by other people, or for that matter caused by events. What appear to be external attacks are really internal reactions. This can often be a difficult pill to swallow. It goes against many of our belief systems and much of our self-image. Not only do we blame others for what befalls us, but we feel that we know what they need to do to "fix" *their* problems. It is a bit like trying to put a new roof on someone else's house when ours is the one that is leaking. Our feelings and moods are not the fault of someone or something else. We are solely responsible for all of our moods and responses.

If you do not believe that you cause 100% of the dumping in your life, then at least understand that you manifest about 90-95% of the dumping you experience. At any rate, how do we learn to break free of these traps? We can learn to break free by catching ourselves when we begin to step into one and then choosing a different path. We can also use this phrase: **It seems that life dumps on me enough, so don't dump on myself.**

Alternative Ways to Perceive and Create

What would your life be like if you were able to knock 90-95% of the dumping that is in it, out of it? We can achieve this by choosing how we respond to life events.

I received a letter from a friend one time. She wrote that she had gotten a flat tire while driving with her young children on a little traveled rural road and what a blessing it was. I thought, "A flat tire…a blessing? This ought to be interesting." She explained that she got a flat tire and pulled off to the side of the road wondering what to do next. When along this little-traveled road came a car with a man driving. He stopped and changed the flat tire for her. She felt "blessed" that another car came along, that he stopped even though he was a complete stranger and that he was able to change her tire. She probably also learned a few things about changing a flat. So now, was this a "bad" experience or a "good" experience? Many would look at a flat tire as a bad experience, but she didn't. And we can look at this type of experience as a positive one as well.

As an aside, many times I have told this story of my friend with a flat tire to both friends and clients over the years. One day a patient came in to my office all excited. He said he was on his way home from culinary school when he got a flat tire. He was a well-built young man over six feet tall. He related how he had gotten a flat tire while driving. When he pulled his car over and checked he realized that he did not have a spare tire. He began to get angry. He then remembered the flat tire story I told him and he chose to not be angry. He said to himself that he had been wanting to get in some jogging lately, but had not had time. He chose to not dump on himself. He realized as we had previously discussed that **All problems are opportunities.** So he decided to turn this into an opportunity rather than a problem. His home was only a few miles away and he began jogging with a smile on his face. This by itself would have made a wonderful story, but then something else happened. He had barely gotten started jogging when a car pulled up next to him and asked if the car with the flat was his. He responded "yes" and the man asked him if he would like a ride home. He accepted the offer and was dropped off a few minutes later at his front door. The patient said he was certain that if he had stormed down the street on foot with an angry look on his face that the man would never have stopped.

A life crisis, as it is often referred to, does not come in to our lives because it is meant for us to suffer. Rather, it is an opportunity that often contains pain. The pain may be of a physical, psychological or emotional nature or may contain components of two or all three. It becomes a problem when we only focus on the pain aspect of it and fail to see the opportunity that exists within it. Neale Donald Walsch states that, "pain is an experience, suffering is a judgment made about that experience." These life crises are life presentations that pull us out of our day-to-day existence and lift us up to a higher level of functioning and ability. They challenge us to learn and to grow.

What I heard about problems many years ago is still so appropriate. Learn to make your burdens your blessings. All dark clouds do have silver linings. We just have to open our eyes to see them. If you look and still cannot find them, then you are not looking hard enough. Blame and self-blame deepen a wound, whereas taking responsibility and making corrections begins the healing process and creates growth.

If we can take a "bad" experience and gain knowledge, benefits and awareness, then is it really a "bad" experience? I would propose that it isn't, and in fact I would call it a good experience. So, if we can take the 5-10% that we labeled as "life dumping on us" and gain something good from it, then it wouldn't be life dumping on us. That would leave us with little or no dumping occurring in our lives. We just need to think about life in a different way. **As we change our thoughts, so shall we change our world.** It is a very empowering place to come from. The reason for this is that our outside world is simply a reflection of the inside world that we have created. Marcus Aurelius Antonius was well aware of this when he stated, "Our life is what our thoughts make it." Life does not have to be something that just happens to us.

How we think about life determines what we see. Our thoughts do determine the world around us. Poet Ralph Waldo Emerson declared that, "Great men are they who see that the spiritual is stronger than any material force; that thoughts rule the world."

We can get an even clearer picture of this if we consider the perspective that life is made up of what we describe as positive, negative and neutral events. There is only one factor that determines which category a life event falls into. And that is our viewpoint. It all depends on how we perceive things…and nothing else. For example, I am an avid vinyl record collector. To search through some dusty old bins in a used record store and possibly unearth some treasure that I have been seeking for decades is very exciting to me. My wife, on the other hand, thinks there isn't much on the planet more boring than that. She sees it as a negative and I see it as a positive event. We could imagine categorizing divorce as a negative, but if one of the spouses was severely physically abusing the other, most people would say it was positive to get out of the marriage. Eating at a Chinese restaurant, getting fired from a job, losing a game, getting married, winning the lottery, having a parent die, a rainy day…all of these and everything else in the world are perceived as positive, negative and neutral based on an individual's viewpoint. Even a shoe falls into this system. When it is on your foot and used for walking it is positive. When someone is kicking you with one I expect most people would call it negative.

I remember reading a letter in a newspaper column a number of years ago. The woman in the letter spoke about how she complained for forty years about her husband's snoring. She then related that her husband passed away a year ago and that there has not been a day that has gone by where she has not wished she could hear his snoring again. This clearly shows how the label we place on something can be a determining factor on how we perceive it and experience it. Imagine it as a coin that we are in control of. Standing on its edge it is a neutral. On one side it is positive and on the other side it is negative. There is no coin toss that leaves us at the mercy of fate. We actually get to determine how we will perceive it. **One person's trash is another person's treasure. One person's pain is another person's pleasure.**

We require interpretation to gain awareness. These interpretations are processed through our memory banks containing our individual history of experience. This accounts for the reason why a single event can occur and there can be as many varied interpretations of the event as there are people observing it.

Begin to notice how many times during the day you have a negative thought, speak a negative word or do a negative action. Actually, make a list and do check marks. I think you will be surprised. Then start reducing the number of negatives you are producing. While you are doing this there is another tool that can also help. This tool is applied by following up with a positive, for each negative that you find yourself producing.

Here is another approach you can use. Consider assuming this viewpoint: nothing is truly negative. And I really do mean nothing. Every event or occurrence in our lives is an opportunity for growth. That is what our existence on this planet is all about.

The following are some examples of how a person can choose to see the good and positive in things when the general tendency might be to see it in a negative way:

When you are ready to complain about the bills you have to pay, instead recognize that you should give thanks for all those who were willing to provide the product or service first and let you pay them later.

When you are ready to complain about the cold weather (or hot weather) outdoors, instead recognize that you should give thanks that you have a warmer (or cooler) indoors in which to go.

When you are ready to complain about the slow driver in front of you, instead recognize that you should give thanks for the opportunity to practice patience.

When you are ready to complain about the unattractive clothes that someone is wearing, instead recognize that you should give thanks for your sight.

When you are ready to complain about not having enough time for things, instead recognize that you should give thanks for having a full life.

When you are ready to complain about washing dirty dishes, instead recognize that you should give thanks for having had food to eat.

We need to try and stay in a constant state of awareness about people, places and events around us. There is a positive side to everything, if we will only look for it. In order to take control of our perceptions and choices and get optimal benefit in creating a positive life we need to recognize our role as creator. If we do not see ourselves as the creator of the events in our life, then we should at least see ourselves as the creator of how we perceive those events.

Another tool I recommend is that we share the "life dumps" phrase with those around us. Tell them we want to stop a lot of the dumping we are doing on ourselves and on those around us. Ask them to help us if they catch us playing the dumping-on-ourselves game. They should ask us gently, "Are you dumping on yourself right now?" This can make us more aware of it and provide an opportunity to break free of those patterns.

What is most important here is breaking free of these traps. They are past programming and they rob us of being in the moment. Therefore, it is of vital importance that when we spot ourselves dumping on ourselves, or someone poses the question to us, that we then stop, assess and evaluate the situation, and acknowledge "the truth" immediately. This is what frees us from our self-imposed prison. We stop the game that our mind plays with us. Remember, **The truth shall set you free.** We become more free and more in control. We become the decider. We do not allow our past history to make the decision for us. The more we express the truth, the whole truth and nothing but the truth, the more free we will be. Truth is to the soul, as the morning sun is to the flower in the meadow.

The power of an individual can be measured by the individual's power over oneself. The more we stop dumping on ourselves, the more we do not need to prove that we are right. The more we break free of unhealthy patterns and programs, the more aware that we become. We then come to truly know ourselves. The Chinese philosopher, Lao-Tzu, often regarded as the founder of Taoism, observed, **"He who knows others is learned, he who knows himself is enlightened."**

So, in order to have other people help us break free and become more conscious, and to make it go as smoothly as possible I suggest several points. One, that the "helper" approach "the dumper" as gently as possible. It is important to do this with kindness and consideration so that it does not set off the dumper. Second, it can also be done with the slightest bit of humor in your voice (if it helps) the other person. One method may work better with one person, but with a second person you have to use the other method. Ask the person first, before a situation even occurs, what they think will work best for them to not set off their defense mechanisms. Then use whatever works best.

The Formation of the Mindfield

We all have defense mechanisms in our mind that we use to "protect" ourselves. To the person or helper trying to enter into your space it is like a field around you where all these hidden land mines have been placed. One wrong step by the helper, such as a bad choice of words or a wrong tone of voice, and you can explode. I will bet that every one of us has experienced both sides of this situation. I call this area around us a "mindfield". I would more specifically define it this way. The **mindfield** is an area around an individual that is made up of both conscious and subconscious over-reactions and triggers (formed from programming, past events and traumas), and defense mechanisms that the mind employs in the generally mistaken belief that they protect the individual. I will discuss a way to approach the mindfield in greater detail later. For now, suffice it to say that the two most gentle approaches are "the question" and "humor." If you suggest to a person that he is dumping on himself and he becomes angry and hostile and can not handle hearing it, then you might want to head for a foxhole because explosions from the mindfield are likely to follow. What the mindfield does not fully destroy it takes prisoner. The most long-term prisoner in this jail is ourself. **Ironically, the mindfield**

cripples the very person it is designed to protect. As the poet John Milton reminded us, "The mind…can make a heav'n of hell, [or] a hell of heav'n."

It is important to understand a bit more about the mindfield and defense mechanisms because it can help us to comprehend why we act the way we do at times. It also helps us to see how we avoid true reality and create separation between ourselves and others.

Defense mechanisms are mental devices or reactions to conflict or frustration that individuals use to protect themselves from emotional conflict, perceived dangers and external stressors in order to enhance their self-concept or image. Defense mechanisms are formed by the ego (a part of the mind) and serve the purpose of reducing tension and anxiety, but are typically self-deceptive in nature. With use they become relatively habitual and instinctual. The frequency, severity and rigidity of their use generally determine the degree to which they are detrimental. Although some defense mechanisms are useful, at times the awareness and growth that they rob us of costs us dearly. That is the essence of their maladaptive nature.

Listed below are some of the primary defense mechanisms that we employ in life. These are some of the ways that a person attempts to deal with emotional conflict or internal or external stressors:

Denial is the refusal to admit some painful or discomforting aspect of subjective experience or external reality that others would find evident and obvious.

Devaluation is the assigning of exaggerated negative qualities to oneself or someone else.

Displacement is the transferring of a feeling about one object onto a substitute object that is typically less threatening.

Intellectualization is the extensive use of abstract thinking or the making of generalizations in order to eliminate, control or decrease disturbing feelings.

Passive Aggression is having a hidden hostility, resistance, or resentment that lies behind an appearance of open compliance, so that a person indirectly and unassertively expresses their aggression toward others. This often occurs in situations where individuals are in subordinate positions and feel they have no other way to more openly express their assertiveness.

Projection is the process of taking one's own unacceptable impulses, thoughts or feelings and falsely attributing them to another person or group.

Rationalization is the providing of incorrect explanations for one's own self-interest in order to conceal the real reasons for one's feelings, thoughts, words or actions.

Reaction Formation is the process of perceiving one's own feelings and thoughts as unacceptable and so substituting thoughts, feelings or behaviors that are the complete opposite.

Repression is the process of banishing one's unpleasant or distressing thoughts, memories, experiences or wishes from the conscious mind to the subconscious mind.

Sublimation is the channeling of potentially negative impulses or feelings into a more socially acceptable behavior. A person having aggressive impulses, for example, may become a boxer or infantryman.

Suppression is the conscious effort to avoid thinking about distressing wishes, thoughts, experiences, memories or problems.

Control of the Mind

You can see where the ego is quite clever and devious with the tools it has created to control you. There are times when the defense mechanisms listed above can prove useful. However, they prevent us from confronting and facing in an honest way the feelings, thoughts, words, actions, memories, impulses, experiences and wishes that we have. This routinely prevents and sabotages our growth and freedom as a human being. These are mechanisms that the mind convinces us to use in order to keep us from the truth in life situations. I believe that we can benefit greatly by beginning to dismantle these mechanisms or at least bring them under our conscious control. We need to quiet the mind and it's endless chatter because it puts a wall between each present moment and us. Stopping the mind's constant droning will start to address this problem. **If we do not control the mind then it will control us.**

There is one aspect about the link, that we as human beings have with our minds, that I find very fascinating and astonishing. That is, how would we react if another person tried to control our life with the degree of control that our mind does? How would you handle it if someone tried to control you with their selfish, deceitful, possessive, destructive, dictatorial ways? You would probably call them insidious and evil, and do everything in your power to free yourself from their control. It would likely become your life's mission, if it were necessary to do so.

I also suggest that we teach people how to work their way through our mindfield. For example, if you say something to me in such-and-such a way (i.e., using these type of words and this tone of voice) it will be the most effective way of getting your message in without setting off my mindfield. By putting these procedures in place we can begin the process of letting go of the fear that keeps the mindfield active and armed. Your mind will not appreciate you taking back control. **As the mind is angry**

for what it has lost, the soul is smiling for what it has found.

Reducing the power we allow the mind to have over us begins with a better understanding of how we operate. Let us go back once more to the concept of positive, negative and neutral events. If we are (a) taking a neutral event (which all events are) and (b) having thoughts related to that event or making judgments on that event, then (c) placing a negative or "bad" label on the event and (d) following this up with a negative mood, attitude or emotion, then we are surely creating this negativity around ourselves. This is why Guy Finley, author of "The Secret of Letting Go", wrote, "**Unhappiness does not come at you, it comes from you**." Recognize that only you can take yourself out of a state of happiness or joy and only you can put yourself into a state of gloom or anger. Each time that we carry out this four-step procedure we are bringing negativity into our world. I am not saying we have no right to do it or that we should not do it. I am simply saying that we need to recognize that we are doing it. If we chose to think this way, and see the world this way, then it is a world of our creation. What we view in our lives is a product of what we think and believe. It is all based on how we process the world. A person or event in the world is not the source of our misery. Our misery is an outcome of what and how we choose to think and believe, which then shapes who we are. Life in a sense is like one big Rorschach Inkblot. We project onto life what is in our mind and thoughts. **As we think so shall we see. As we see so shall we be.** The question to our self becomes…does this action or pattern help to create the world that I want.

The Recognition and Removal of Thought Distortions

Not satisfied with creating the unhappiness in our life, we take this mental patterning one step further. The pattern that we have chosen and created we then use as a way to validate and verify to others and ourselves that life is dumping on us. Furthermore, we will use it as proof, and a reason to justify our negative treatment of those people, things or events associated with it. When this is firmly locked into our way of living it results in stereotyping and biases. We interpret something about one or several events and we then assume it is that way with every similar event. If a car dealer cheated us then all car dealers are dishonest. If we lose our job then all bosses are out to get us. If a friend betrays our trust then nobody can be trusted.

When we perceive the world through these patterns we are distorting the truth. We often make assumptions and yet report them as though they are facts. A fact is something that is known to be true or real. A belief implies a mental acceptance of something as being true even though absolute certainty may not be present. An assumption is a supposition or belief that is not based on positive knowledge or absolute certainty, but rather on what seems valid, true or probable in one's own mind. Misrepresentations of assumptions as facts create more direct and indirect chaos, conflict and confusion in our lives than we can possibly imagine. We too often then take an assumption and jump to a conclusion. It is the truth that sets us free. We will never be fully free until we can see the world in a distortion-free manner. In a book I read back in the late 60's, the author Robert Heinlein described a character as being a "Fair Witness." This character was a trained professional who was primarily hired to be an observer during legal or business transactions. If necessary the witness could later go to court and report the facts they observed. They were trained to see things pure and unadulterated. An example in the book was when the Fair Witness was asked to describe what color a house in the distance was painted. The Fair Witness stated that, "It's white on this side." She made no inference or assumption as to how the other sides were painted because she was unable to see the other sides. To say that the house was painted white would be to make a statement not supported by fact. She just observed and reported, "What is."

I believe this approach allows us to see the world and the people in it in a much more true way. That does not mean we should not make assumptions and inferences, it is just that they should be presented as such. **The more we are able to see things in front of us as they actually are in the moment, the more in the moment we actually are ourselves.**

How do we handle fact versus opinions? In general, when you are presented with an opinion, feel free to discuss it. When you are presented with a fact, accept it and deal with it.

Once we recognize that we create distortions in our thinking the next step is to determine what we can do to change this process. I view this as a five-step procedure.

Procedure for Removing Thought Distortions

1. Identify the emotion you experienced.
2. Examine the event or situation that brought about that emotion.
3. Describe the thought process that occurred during and/or after the event or situation.
4. Find the distortions that were present in the thought process.
5. Dispute and disprove the negative thinking or distortions.
6. Make an accurate restatement of the event or situation.

As we remove our distortions we begin to experience the world without the misinterpretations and falsehoods. **If we wish to know the truth, we must be open to the truth.** It can come to us in any form and at any time. Truth can just as easily come from the words written on subway walls and tenement halls as from the books of religion or from tomes of knowledge. Be prepared to recognize truth in all its forms.

If removing distortions in our thoughts is a worthwhile project then we should begin with the following concept about our thought process in which we tend to take great pride. We tend to hold a view that thinking is the process that separates us from what we call lower life forms. While that statement may hold truth, it is not the factor that we should most prize in ourselves. That is because our true power does not lie in our thinking, it lies in our consciousness. At higher levels of being it is our consciousness that rules. Look at it this way. **Consciousness can exist without thought, but thought can not exist without consciousness.** Therefore, seeking consciousness is ultimately a much more important goal than spending admiring our greater ability to think. By focusing on our consciousness, it puts us in touch with the highest level of who we are.

The Source of All Negative Emotion

In order to be open to the truth it necessitates that we move away from fear. It has been said that there are really only two emotions in the universe. All other emotions are subsumed under one or the other of these categories. The two emotions are love and fear. Think about this. If this view is correct and if we took steps to wipe out all the fear in our world then what would be left is love. That would be a very interesting world indeed.

How do we rid ourselves of the fears we have? It actually is simpler than one would expect. Consider a fear of water. Person A will go into the water up to his neck and is willing to bob his head under the water very quickly. He has a fear of the water, but it does not greatly impact on him or control him. Person B will go in up to his neck, but will not put his head under the water because of his fear ("You can't breathe down there, you know."). Person C will only go in up to his waist ("I'm not getting more than half my body in there."). Person D will go in up to his ankles ("Hey, leave me alone. I'm in the water aren't I."). Person E will only stand on the beach, but will not go in the water ("I can experience it from here. Besides, it's colder than I like."). Person F is in town with his friends on a warm summer day and someone suggests that they should all go to the beach. Everyone excitedly agrees except for Person F. He stammers, "Oh my, look at the time. I just remembered I was supposed to go to…uh…help…yes, help my father…yeah, help him do…I mean clean …the…uh…garage. I've got to help him with it now. I'll see you guys later, okay." Person F has so much fear about the water that he is not even willing to face looking at it. This fear greatly controls his life. It controls it to such an extent that it now has a negative impact on his social life. How many of us have fears that affect us in some significant negative way?

The common denominator with these fears, as with all fears, is our unwillingness to face them. **The degree to which we are unwilling to confront something is directly proportional to the control we allow it to have over us.** Therefore, how do we go about gaining greater control of our lives? We confront whatever it is. Person F needs to quit avoiding the water. He should go to the beach, then step in up to his ankles and work his way up to his waist and so on. Then he should take some swimming lessons and maybe even get his lifeguard certificate. At that point he would have no fear of the water. His fear would be gone completely. He would become more powerful and have greater control over his life. Confronting our fears is very likely the single greatest growth-producing action that can be done as a human being. I believe there is nothing we can do that can give us greater personal freedom, awareness and growth. **Do not fear a challenge, rather challenge a fear.**

Be receptive to a new challenge. If we should chose to have a fear regarding the future our fear should never be that we aim too high, but rather that we aim too low. A person should never be satisfied to crawl when they possess the ability to walk. To paraphrase Abraham Lincoln: things may come to those who wait, but only what's left by those who took action. Fear not a new challenge. Recognize that it is an invitation. Accept it with open arms. If you see truth and expanded awareness in it then take up the challenge. **Familiarity can bring comfort, but unfamiliarity can bring growth.** Do not allow your fear to rule you or prevent you from making a contribution that helps yourself and/or others. Every person has talent and something to contribute. The difficulty often lies in being willing to face the fear in the darkness of uncertainty until you emerge into the light. To not do so is to hide, and every form of refuge has its price. Do not fear a struggle or a challenge. Embrace it. Do not fear expanding your awareness and your world. There is so much growth to be gained even when we may risk experiencing pain, discomfort or suffering. Those sufferings will always pass. Find the value in all that happens to you. I find it helpful to remember, that it was once said, **"One can learn more from ten days of agony than ten years of contentment."**

It is fear that always holds us back. It is only necessary to remember one thing in order to recognize the full power of fear. **The source of all negative emotion is fear.** If we have only two primary emotions in the universe and they are love and fear, and love we associate as a synonym for God, then fear would seem to be the synonym for the devil. So possibly what many religious people describe as the devil, or as the work of the devil, may be fear. We may, for instance, steal, kill, commit adultery or bear false witness because of our jealousy and greed or, more accurately, out of our fear that we would not be able to get what we want any other way. **The greatest thief of all is fear, for it robs one of life's most precious gem…love.**

It is interesting to recognize the pattern that fear has. Something occurs and then we create fear where there once was none. Thus, we bring fear into existence and give it life. Once we give fear life we then try to avoid it which attracts the fear to us and it begins to take control over it's very creator. We go from being the cause of the fear to being the effect of the fear. Fear takes on a life of its own. When we resist dealing with our fear it causes it to continue because the only way of alleviating fear is to confront it. **Resistance creates persistence.** Also, be aware that resistance is actually fear in disguise.

First we should interpret any fear that we experience as a warning. Then we should see it as a motivator in order to confront it, take action or understand it instead of seeing it as an automatic inhibitor. When we fear something we make it larger and more powerful than it really is. Which is why by confronting it, we can overcome it. We see the truth of it, rather than what our fear builds it up to be. Again, it's the truth that sets us free.

If we were able to bring ourselves to fully confront all aspects of life a fascinating process would begin to occur. Our negative emotions would disappear. I expect that the level of joy and happiness we would experience would be unimaginable. **Unhappiness is the consequence of being unwilling to confront and accept that which is.** The unhappiness that we create in our lives is always based on some aspect of resistance, fear and not accepting that which is. The degree of unhappiness correlates to the amount of resistance we have to the person, situation or event that we are not accepting. When the unhappiness is occurring with our thoughts it is the result of a judgment, and when it is occurring as an emotion it is the result of some component of negativity.

The light of consciousness causes the shadows of fear to disappear. We need to bring the fear into our conscious awareness and not be afraid of it. It really can not harm us unless we allow it to. Either: (1) just allow it to be there, (2) use rational thinking to overpower and overcome it or (3) embrace it.

When we allow our fear to just be there, it automatically reduces the level of the fear. Eventually the fear goes away. Think about it. By it's very nature we have to be afraid of it in order for it to persist.

In the vast majority of incidents where we experience fear, it is irrational and illogical. We are simply over-reacting to a situation. If we allow it to overwhelm us, then we put ourselves in an even worse situation. Therefore, by using logical, rational thinking we can put it into a better perspective and create a healthier, more effective place from which to operate.

We can also embrace the fear. It may sound silly, but by doing this, it reduces the power that we allow the fear to have over us. Stop and think for a moment. How can we truly be afraid of something that we are willing to embrace? If it does not take the fear away entirely, it will significantly diminish it.

When we label people, things or events as negative it is because we tend to fear them as a result of our past history with them (which usually contained negative moods and negative consequences for us). Although we would quickly argue that we would prefer to have a positive rather than a negative, we should remember that like photography, if you know what to do with a negative you can turn it into a positive and create a wonderful picture. Consequently, we should not fear the negatives, but rather learn how to develop and process them.

Fear is not all bad. It does serve a purpose. It tells us that we are avoiding some aspect of ourselves. Anxiety and mental anguish are both derived from fear. We often experience them when we encounter something that we do not fully confront.

When we do not see the truth in something or someone it creates a distortion of the truth. It causes us to make inaccurate observations and false assumptions, which then leads to unfair conclusions and judgments. This distortion process begins as a result of not having some particular knowledge about the item, person or event. This "not knowing" about something can occur on both conscious and subconscious levels. **If a distortion is not based on not knowing then it is based on fear.** If we fear something we are not seeing the truth about it, and this fear is often based on our past history.

The most powerful negative force in our lives is fear. Up to this point it has ruled the world. Not only in the way countries act and react toward each other, but how we interact with people around us. Most important for us to realize is exactly what we do to ourselves with our fear. We need to recognize how much it negatively impacts on who we are.

We perceive fear as a warning, which is true, it is a warning. The problem begins, however, with how we react to fear when it occurs. When fear arrives we *believe* it means we should leave. We think that we should back away and retreat. Actually, we should do just the opposite and confront it. Fear causes us to withdraw and slip further into the physical world. Whenever we experience fear it lowers our vibrational rate. Prove this to yourself. Think of something that you are really fearful of. Get into the fear deeply and feel how it begins to affect your body. You will probably cringe and pull the body in on itself, increasing the sensation of density and heaviness. Now, go take on that fear. Confront it and overcome it. Now examine how you feel. Notice that you feel more alert and aware. You feel brighter and lighter. That lightness you feel is an increase in your vibrational rate. It is releasing you a bit more from the constraints of the physical world. **Our fears are the weights that hold us down from attaining our true heights.**

Fear has had a profound impact on who we are. Because of our urge to avoid it or to beat a hasty retreat, fear has done us great harm. We trade in our consciousness and our growth when we keep our distance from fear. If you find that, at present, you feel unable to operate without there being fear in your life, then accept it for the moment and just be courageous. Continue to confront the fears and do not give in to them. Mark Twain once wrote that, "Courage is mastery of fear – not absence of fear." Everything we do makes us stronger for the next challenge we face.

The role of fear in our lives should not be underestimated. **We are damaged more by our fears than by all the mishaps, misfortunes and mistakes we have ever experienced. To overcome a fear we must come to embrace it.**

We do not know how high we are capable of reaching as a human being. Fear is one of the principal elements that keep us from achieving all that we want in this world. If we can begin to recognize what holds us back we can begin to change our world. **Fear, procrastination and inertia are the three primary barriers to creation, achievement and success.** They paralyze us. Being half-sure, but attempting something anyway, is called confidence. Needing to be 100 percent sure is called procrastination.

It is ironic that what holds us back from tackling and overcoming our fears is fear. We have fear of not overcoming it. A fear of succumbing to it. It is a fear of failure. We fear taking on our fear. President Franklin Delano Roosevelt said, "We have nothing to fear, but fear itself." How true that is. From a similar perspective Wayne Dyer points out that, "Fear itself does not exist in the world. There are only fearful thoughts and avoidance behaviors."

So let's challenge ourselves and tackle our fears. The very worst that would happen is that we try and we fail. Is that really so bad? Is it as bad as not trying at all? Even failure has value. **We can learn as much from failure as we do from success.** As Deepak Chopra points out, "In the rubble of devastation and disaster are buried hidden treasures."

Henry Ford, who was always admired for his creative ideas and applications recognized this when he said, **"Failure is only the opportunity to begin again more intelligently."**

I have observed several interesting details about fear. One is that **More harm is caused by fearing than is caused by the object of our fear.** Second, is that **All fears are parasites. They possess no power except that which we give to them.** Where this is most noticeable is when we actually work to rid ourselves of a fear. Picture all your fears as a gang encircling you. You decide to take the biggest baddest one and knock him to the ground. All the rest of the gang then backs up a few steps. Similarly, when we tackle one fear and defeat it, it causes the other fears to lose some of their power. This is because they get all of their power from us. By the act of defeating the fear we become stronger, our other fears become weaker and we therefore, become more able to defeat any other fears.

It is also important to note the genesis of fear. Each fear is based in a belief and generally it is a distorted belief. As Harry Palmer wrote, **"Fear is a belief in our inadequacy to deal with something."** Consequently, it becomes imperative that we recognize and expand our ability to conquer fear by confronting it.

The Fallacy of Failure

I often say to patients, "I was noticing when you came into my office today what a great walker you are." They look a little befuddled and I say, "I'll bet you rarely fall down." They respond, "That's true" and I continue. "I'll bet you weren't always such a great walker. In fact, I'll bet that when you were young you fell down a lot. Probably hundreds and thousands of times, but you didn't give up. You persisted and now here you are a great walker." If only we would tackle the challenges in our lives now with the same perseverance.

True failure only occurs when you give up. It states in the Koran that, "God helps those who persevere." As long as we do not quit we still have the opportunity to succeed. We need to keep our eye on the tracks and our feet on the rails. **If we allow our train to stop at failure, we will never reach our destination of success.** Once you give up you will never know if success was right beyond the next bend in the road. As long as you keep trying and adapt to any changes in the road, you cannot fail. Victor Hugo expressed this concept when he said, **"A bend in the road is not the**

end of the road unless you fail to make the turn."

What works best for me is to assume this viewpoint: **There is no such thing as failure. There is only *(1)* the learning experience or *(2)* giving up.** So, if you have learned something, then you have succeeded. We need to realize that making mistakes is part of the learning process. Whenever we make a mistake we have two options. One is to beat ourselves up over it. The other is to choose to see the mistakes as an opportunity. We can learn from it if we recognize that a mistake is nothing more than a part of the process that shows us where a correction needs to be made. I will go further into this corrective process later in the book.

If we do not change the way we define failure, then we at least need to change the way we look at it. I believe that: **If a person is wise enough to lift the mask of failure, they will find beneath it the face of success.**

The Problem Solving Approach

In order to increase the likelihood of success at life tasks, approaching problems in a methodical and yet creative way is extremely beneficial. I use a seven-step problem solving approach. I call the first three steps of this the Problem Solving Tree. This is because if mapped out on paper it would look like a detailed outline of a tree with all its branches. Whether used to solve a present-time problem or used to prepare for an upcoming discussion it would look the same.

The first three steps of this approach are (1) define the problem or issue, (2) "brainstorm" possible solutions to the problem and (3) determine what the consequences would be of each possible solution. Brainstorm means to think up as many solutions as you can no matter how unusual, untried, unrealistic or illogical they may seem. At this step of the process you do not rule anything out. Just keep listing them.

The trunk of the tree would be the question that is posed. Each main branch would be one possible option. Each secondary branch would be a response or consequence of each main branch. Each secondary branch would also have even smaller limbs branching off from it. This would continue all the way down to a twig. I visualize it this way: I am unhappy at my job and wonder what I should do about it. The tree trunk becomes "What should I do about the unhappiness I feel about my job?" The main branches might be (a) quit my job and find another one, (b) tell my boss how I feel and see if it is possible to get a different position within the company, (c) learn to live with it and (d) determine if it is certain parts of the job I dislike, and if so, see if I can change those tasks. Each one of these main branches diverges or forks off into smaller branches. Once I have all my main branches in place I go back to the first main branch (quit my job) and attach my smaller branches by examining what the consequences would be if I quit my job. Each consequence becomes a new smaller branch attached to a main branch. I look at all the pros and cons of each of these secondary branches. One of these secondary branches may be, for example, "I may not find another job quickly and would have no money to pay bills." If we take one of these secondary branches, such as, "I may have to move out of my home if I have no money to pay for it" and explore the consequences of that, we will attach even smaller branches to the secondary branch. An example of this level branch might be "If I had to move out because I had no money I would have to find a place to live."

I would repeat this procedure until I had exhausted all possibilities for all branches. I would then have, to the best of my ability, a complete outline down to the smallest twig of what the options and consequences would be in solving the problem about my unhappiness on the job.

I also use this tree format to prepare for some conversations or discussions that I am going to have with someone. I would use this if it were, for instance, a delicate situation where I want to use the right words. It is a way of practicing or role-playing. It can be used to visualize or rehearse a particular situation that we do not initially feel confident about. A person might use it to prepare answers to potential questions they might encounter in going to a job interview. Its use is unlimited.

You might think, "Hey, I can't do this every time I have a problem to solve. It would take too long." Actually, it may seem that way at first, but the more you use the problem solving tree and the full seven-step approach below, the faster it works. This is because we begin to format or program the mind into thinking this way. Plus, we have extra time on our hands anyway because we are not spending so much time repairing damage from frequently-made poor choices. Furthermore, most problems we run into in life are not new problems. They tend to be exactly like, or similar to, other problems we have had. When we take the time to increase the odds of making a good choice on an issue or problem we can typically use that as a template, prototype or archetype to use with similar problems or situations. So in the long run we actually can save time. The added bonus is that life generally goes better for ourselves and others as the result of well thought-out, conscious choices.

Before I discuss the seven-step problem solving approach let me point out what I call the zero step. This step takes place before you even begin to solve the problem. The zero step is: "0. Who owns the problem? Or what part of the problem is yours?"

I believe that we should not be solving problems that are not ours to solve. We should work on our own problems and allow other people the opportunity of solving their own problems. If we solve their problems for them then they never get to be good problem solvers themselves. By all means let's help them if they ask for our help, but we should serve only as a guide in order to assist them. This should be done in the same way that a good parent helps their child with their homework. Don't do the work for them by giving them the answers. At the very least do not do any more than you need to do in order for them to find all the possible solutions and consequences to their problem.

If you are talking on the phone to a friend and you cannot hear because your kids are in front of you fighting over a toy, do you have a problem (zero step)? Yes, you're right. You do. Unfortunately, many people would say their problem was the kids fighting over the toy, but that is not the problem. Your problem is you cannot hear your friend on the phone. So don't try to solve the problem of who gets the toy. You might say to the kids to either stop arguing or take their argument into another room because you cannot hear on the phone. Of course, the best solution would be to give them a copy of the problem solving approach and have them go work out a solution.

The Problem Solving Approach

0. Who owns the problem? What part of the problem is yours?
1. Define the problem or issue and be specific.
2. "Brainstorm" as many solutions to the problem as possible.
3. Examine what the consequences would be for each solution.
4. Choose the best solution(s).
5. Implement the solution(s).
6. After a reasonable period of time, evaluate the effectiveness of the solution.
7. If the solution is working then the problem is done with. If it is not working go back to step two and follow the same procedure.

Suppose I had a young son, Johnny, who comes to me and says that Eddie in school keeps picking on him and starting fights. I would sit Johnny down and pull out my problem-solving sheet, get some blank paper and say, "Okay let's look for some solutions." Using step one we would define the problem as, "I don't like it when Eddie picks on me and starts fights with me in school." Then on step two I would ask Johnny what he thinks he could do to solve the problem. He responds, "I could run away from him." "I could tell the teacher on him." "I could run to big Roger to protect me." "I could get some other kids to beat him up." "I could take a gun to school and shoot him." I know it is shocking to see this last one on the list, but one of the rules of brainstorming is that you write down everything that is given to you. I will show shortly why this is so important.

I would help guide Johnny with my questions toward any other options I could think of that he had not already given me. In doing this, remember that I do not want to give him any more help than is necessary. Giving no help would be best, but if my assistance is required then giving him 1% help and allowing him to get the rest that would be the optimum situation. If he did not get them all I would keep increasing the amount of guidance I give until he does. My 1% questions might be something like; "Can you think of any other possible solutions you have not already told me?" A 10% question may be, "Can you think of anyone else who might be able to help?" A 30% may be, "Are there any other adults at school who could help?" A 70% question might be, "Do you think your principal could help?" I would do this individually for each option he had not thought of. I would increase my guidance by very small increments, so as not to rob him of any independent learning.

Moving on to step three we would pick the first option and discuss the pros and cons of implementing it. I would guide and use increments with these consequences just as I did with the options. When we get to the option of taking a gun to school and shooting him, I would question him on the consequences. He might respond with, "That would take care of my problem" and I would agree. Then as he thought of the negative consequences he might say "Gee, maybe the other kids wouldn't want to hang around with me anymore. Maybe I would have to go to prison. I wouldn't be able to live here anymore or be with my friends anymore. Boy, that wouldn't be a very good solution." The wonderful thing about this is that "he" decides that it is not a good solution. He chooses to not want to do that type of behavior. He learns that there are better ways to deal with problems.

It is interesting to note that step three (the consequences step) is the step that most people leave out when they have situations arise. This omission seems to be particularly true for many children and teenagers. They often act without thinking of the possible consequences.

As we finish with the consequences for each possible solution we do step four and Johnny then picks a solution or solutions. He follows step five and goes back to school implementing them. After a period of time we discuss whether the solutions have resolved his problem. If so, the problem is finished. If not, we go back to step two and brainstorm solutions. We look to see if there are solutions that we had not thought of before and add any to the list. Also the circumstances may have changed somewhat, so that new alternatives may now be possible. If we ever get stuck at the brainstorming level we can always seek advice from other sources such as, other kids (what worked for them), older siblings, other parents, teachers, principals, books, guidance counselors, psychologists and so on.

Again, you might be thinking that this process would take too long. However, as we teach this procedure to our children, coworkers, and others (as well as practice and learn it ourselves) we find that these people come to us less frequently with problems. This is because they are solving the problems themselves. It reminds me of the old saying that "A stitch in time saves nine." So if we take the time to put one stitch into the unraveling hem now it will save us doing nine stitches later. It is a more proactive approach to problem solving.

Reasons Why Problems Persist

When we use this problem solving approach long enough we reprogram the mind to the point of where we find ourselves making more effective choices. It becomes more automatic. This does not mean that our responses become more automatic. It means that using the formula becomes automatic. Once you become used to the procedure it is amazing how quickly you can run through a problem. Also any and every problem we have can be plugged into this procedure whether it is a new problem or a recurring one. Recurring problems drain much of our attention, energy and freedom. **The only reason a problem persists is because an individual does not or can not see the truth about it.** When we do not see the truth in the world around us or within us, we are not seeing distortion-free. Not seeing from a distortion-free perspective creates major difficulties within our lives. First of all it can lead us down a false path as to the source of a problem. By not having a good understanding of a problem and its cause, we tend to either do a poor job of solving the problem or never get the problem solved at all. Which then gives persistence to the problems around us. A particular problem, for example, may never seem to go away.

The problem solving approach helps us to make more conscious and deliberate choices. We become more aware and more in-the-moment. We reduce the pattern of choices either being made for us by our mind or being based on an emotionally-laden, traumatic event from our past history. We, therefore, become more at cause and less at effect in our life. We begin to awaken more from our daydream and reduce our unconscious way of living.

When we apply the problem solving approach in conjunction with the arm wrestling technique, the Golden Rule, seek first…, life dumps…and so on (all of which will be discussed shortly), then we are creating SOULutions. It is more than making a choice. **Creating SOULutions requires applying optimum intention in our thoughts, words and actions toward solving a problem in a way that best promotes the spirituality of ourselves and other spiritual beings.**

At times, making the best choice can be very difficult. This is because there are many components and competing forces that make up our personality. Gary Zukav expressed it well in his book "Seat of the Soul". He described the "splintered personality" as having one aspect that may be loving while another aspect may be vindictive. One might be charitable and another selfish. Each aspect has it's own goals and values. The problem lies in not being aware of all those different aspects of our personality, yet at the same time we are attempting to choose our intentions consciously. The aspect of ourselves that wins, in each one of these opposing conflicts is the aspect that is the strongest. The choice made by this aspect of our personality might not, however, always be the best choice. The intention of this strongest aspect, based on its goals and values, will be what our mind then uses to create our reality. At that point we find ourselves in the ineffective and problem-creating position of intending one thing, but then thinking, saying or doing something else. For example, we might wish to see ourselves as charitable, but since our selfishness is stronger it will override our charitableness. Hence, we end up creating a reality that is not what we want. These divisions of the personality create counter-intentions. These counter-intentions work against our spiritual goals of achieving all that we are capable of being. So, we find that our mood is depressed, bored, hopeless or some other lower level feeling. We find ourselves being unhappy with our career, our social life, financial issues and so on. We desire a particular thing, but instead we keep getting more of what we don't want. For these reasons I believe that the problem solving approach can help guide us toward better choices. It can help us to make a choice that is healthier and based on *right* not *might.*

Life is a series of continuous problems. The greatest gift we can give ourselves and others is that of knowing how to be a good problem solver. Although it may seem illogical to think that everything in life is a problem, it is that way. It's just that we have forgotten that they are problems. Walking, talking, dressing, sitting upright, riding a bike, taking a bath, using a fork, tying our shoes, and correctly calculating 2 plus 2 are problems.

Most of us have solved these problems. We just continue to use the same solutions that worked for us in the past and we have gotten so good at these solutions that we no longer even perceive them as problems. **The better we can be at problem solving the more effective we can be at life.**

Many believe that a mentally healthy person has no problems. Not true. All people have problems. One difference that can be used to delineate a mentally unhealthy individual from a mentally healthy one is how they interact with problems. A mentally unhealthy person has a problem and gets stuck in it. A mentally healthy person gets a problem, resolves it (either through their own efforts or with the help of others) and then, of course, moves on to a new problem. In order to create an interesting life it does not require ending all of one's problems, but rather requires moving on to problems that hold more interest and fascination. **One measure of personal power and awareness is the ability to exchange a problem for a more interesting problem.**

What we call problems are actually opportunities. Each and every problem presents us with specific challenges and opportunities to learn, grow and recognize what we can be capable of. Many times we are confronted by a problem that we feel we could not possibly deal with, but after all is said and done we found that we survived it and learned some valuable lessons. Seeing problems as opportunities may not make it any easier to manage the problem, but it can help to make the managing of it, and life itself, more satisfying and interesting.

Perfect Control: The Arm Wrestling Technique

One of the best ways of solving problems, interacting with the world and achieving our goals is using a method that I call the **"Arm Wrestling Technique"**. I teach it this way. I sit next to a patient in my office. I tell them we are going to do some arm wrestling.

I explain that, "This arm wrestling is a metaphor for approaching life, using control and communicating. In life we have goals and obstacles. The same applies to this." I ask, "What are the goals of arm wrestling?" They reply that it is to get the other persons arm and knuckles down. I then say as I grip their hand, "Okay, have your goal in mind. Begin." I allow them to put my hand down quickly. Then I say, "Good, you achieved your goal. You earned your 'A', but did you have to use so much force to do it?" They always reply with something about the fact that they expected me to put up a fight and I didn't do that. They expected resistance. I look them in the face and reply; "Do you often go walking through the world expecting resistance?" Patients respond with a yes most of the time. I say, "Let's do it again and this time see if you can use less force." They do it and again I offer no resistance. They used less force and still won. I say, "You still got your 'A'. Only this time you didn't have to work so hard or study as much for it, but do you think you could have used even less force?" Again, they reply with a yes. I say, "Okay, I want you to turn that sensitivity knob way up. If I use two tons of force and you use two tons and one featherweight who will win?" They respond that they will. I say, "All right then, let's go again" and I again offer no resistance. This time they do much better. I say, "Great. Now remember that once you've moved my arm three or four inches, the weight of your hand alone, accompanied with the law of gravity, will automatically bring my hand down with no effort or force on your part." This time they do it perfectly. The next time I offer semi-resistance all the way down and allow them to win. The time after that I only semi-resist for half of the distance down and the other half I offer no resistance at all. I then say, "Did you notice anything?" They typically say they continued to use force even though I did not use any in the last half. I state, "Okay, let's try it again. This time I want you to adapt to exactly how much force and effort you need to use to accomplish your goal. If you use too little you don't achieve your goal. If you use too much you are wasting energy." We do it again with me varying and shifting the amount of resistance I use on this run-through so that they change and adapt to precisely the amount needed in each moment. I do as many run-throughs as it takes for them to get it. Sometimes, I stop in the middle and tell them, "Increase your sensitivity more. You are still using too much force. Let's start again." Throughout these last run-throughs I encourage them with "good change-up", "nice touch" or "that was just the right amount." Once they get the idea and apply it accurately I say, "That was perfect control." **Perfect control is using the exact amount of energy that it takes to achieve your goal. No more. No less.**

I often say to them, "That's a nice shirt" (or blouse or whatever). "You probably paid about $40.00 for it. If you give me $80.00 I'll get another one for you." They always decline and I ask, "Why." Their response is that they don't want to pay twice as much. I say, "Good. Why pay any more than you need to pay for something. Right?"

I usually then tell them, "I'd like you to come mow my lawn. I like it two inches tall. You can either use my mower or a ruler and scissors. Which do you want to use?" They choose the mower, of course. I ask, "Why?" They point out that the scissors would take too long and use too much energy. I say, "Precisely. Why use more energy, force, time, money or effort than you need to use to accomplish your goals?"

I then give examples of how this applies in real life. I say, "Imagine you're the secretary and I'm the boss." I get right up in the patient's face when I do this and I angrily shake my finger at them. "Where are those reports? They should have been on my desk an hour ago. Look if you can't handle this job there are ten more outside who can." Then I stop, back away and sit down. I say, "If you were actually the secretary how would that make you feel?" They usually reply that they would be angry or upset. I continue, "Correct. Can you imagine someone in that position also feeling resentful?" "*Yes.*" Frustrated?" "*Yes.*" "Vengeful?" "*Yes.*" "Do you think it would make a person want to work real hard for me?" "*No.*" "Exactly. In fact, not only would someone not want to work hard for me, they will probably now work against me. What it creates is resistance." I then tell them: **If you use too much force in life you create hurt, anger, resentment, revenge and resistance. Especially resistance.** It's very difficult to create the kind of wonderful reality you wish for and dream about when you are creating in others all this resistance to your very own goals.

Next I reverse the roles with the patient. "I'm the secretary now and you, the boss, just came by again after yelling at me twenty minutes ago. You now tell me that you are going out to lunch with Amber, another secretary. After you leave, the phone rings. It's your wife and she wants to speak to you. I get a sly look in my eye and say to her that you aren't there and that you left with one of the secretaries and no-o-o-o-o-o you didn't say when you would be back. I can almost sense the little suspicion I planted in your wife's mind."

I ask the patient if they could picture that happening. They say, "Oh, yes." One time one patient even said. "Oh, yes. Because I've done it."

I then suggest a similar scenario where the secretary takes an important message for the boss, but it "accidentally" falls into the waste paper basket. There are innumerable ways this resistance can appear. If it does not create revenge, it almost certainly creates the *urge* to seek revenge. The bottom line is that if you are going through life using too much force to achieve your goals, then you are also creating a network of people who are going to be working against your goals.

So how does a person use the arm wrestling technique? I give the patient several examples. One is this story that I tell patients. "Imagine we are married and have a couple of kids. My goal is to have the kids pick their toys up off the floor."

I say to the kids, "Okay, pick your toys up", but they don't. So, I up the ante. I use a little more force or energy through the tone of my voice and the choice of my words. I say, "Pick your toys up now." They still don't. So, I increase the force a bit more, saying, "Pick the toys up now or there's going to be a punishment." They still don't. I respond with "pick the toys up now or we're not going to the park." The kids now rush to pick up the toys.

I then turn to the patient and ask what would be wrong with me now saying to the kids, "It's good you're picking them up or I would have paddled your little behinds." The patient usually replies with the fact that I'm already achieving my goal so why would I want to run the risk of creating anger, resentment, frustration, revenge and resistance. Why use more force than you need? Why add fuel to the fire? Exactly.

I had a patient one time that came to her appointment very upset over a situation in her home. Her 16 year-old daughter had "informed" the patient that she would not be home until one a.m. The mother told her that she was not allowed to be out until one o'clock, and certainly not on a school night. This began a heated debate that went something like this: "Everyone else is staying out and so am I." "*No, you're not.*" "Yes, I am." "*Well now you can just stay home.*" "You can't make me." "*Yes, I can.*" "Well, you lay one hand on me and I'll report you to Children and Youth Services." The mother didn't know what to do. She told me "I don't know how to handle it. I can't physically restrain her. How do I stop her from doing whatever she wants to do?"

This situation is not just a matter of what should be done. It's more a matter of how did it get here in the first place and what can be done to prevent future similar situations. The woman described her history of discipline with her child over the years. She clearly had been using too much force for many years. Having used up all the heavy artillery in her arsenal she had nothing left to fall back on. Now that she had used her heaviest punishments there was little else to use. The point is that she had begun using too much force too quickly, when she could have been just as effective in the beginning using a gentler approach with her arm wrestling. This would have left her with much more to use now, if necessary. We need to practice subtlety. Use humor. Pose it as a question rather than as a statement or a demand. Use humor. Humor, by the way, releases endorphins, which improves mood.

Medicine has been following a pattern of excessive force with antibiotics that is similar to what the woman had been using with her daughter. Doctors have prescribed stronger and stronger antibiotics to the point of where resistant strains of bacteria are now developing. This leaves us with no method of stopping the new strains. Excessive force creates resistance.

I came from a large family of nine children. So at times there were eleven of us sitting around the dinner table. As would be expected we would sometimes get a little rambunctious. I remember that my father would just give us a look and we would quiet down. Usually that did it. If it didn't, he might say a few words or slightly increase the tone of his voice.

It has been said that the meek shall inherit the Earth. This could lead one to think that a person should be spineless and submissive. This is not true. The dictionary's primary definition of meek is to be patient and mild and not inclined to anger and resentment. I see the arm wrestling technique as aligning with this description. When you use the arm wrestling technique you are coming from love, respect patience and sensitivity. The concept of never using more force than necessary was well illustrated by Joseph Joubert when he said, **"Never cut what you can untie."**

In general, it seems people in our world have become too aggressive. We need to reduce the amount of force being used in the world. Force and aggression just breed more force and aggression. An individual who stays in an abusive relationship is using too little force. The force they need to use, however, may consist of getting help from counselors, a shelter, the police or the courts, rather than a direct confrontation of force by themselves toward the abuser. Similarly, we can also see the flavor of too little thrust or push in someone who is described as unassertive or shy.

I would never say do not be honest and truthful. It's the truth that sets us free. However, what is just as important as speaking the truth is how you speak it. The songwriter Paul Simon expressed a perfect arm wrestling application when he sang, "Just give me some tenderness beneath your honesty." We all want honesty, but it is much more palatable when offered with side dishes of tenderness and love.

How to Really Win

One might assume that if a person always wanted to win then all that would be necessary is to be able to use the most force. Some believe the more force that one uses the more they will win. In effect, they think that might makes right. Well, this assumption not only does not work, but in fact, it more accurately defines a bully. I would point out to them that the arm wrestling technique is not meant to be used by itself, but rather is to be used in conjunction with other guidelines. The arm wrestling is just one piece of the application puzzle. If used alone it would probably result in too much force being used. You could have the world's most powerful engine in your car, but without a steering wheel for guiding your course it would be ineffective for driving and may lead to serious consequences. Similarly, it would be just as ineffective in life. It would be a fast way of getting where you did not want to go. Using more force is not the solution.

It was the excessively forceful thoughts, words and actions that got this planet into all this trouble to begin with.

In order to win in life you have to take into account many other guidelines, such as; **In order to truly win everyone must win.** You are truly not winning if you gain something, but it results in the deaths of many, permanently damages the environment, or loses you a good friend. How can we live with ourselves if we gain our fortune off the misfortune of others? What good would it be to gain the world, but lose your soul?

Someone once said to me that it's okay to watch out for number one, but be careful you don't step in number two. We all know some people who spend so much time watching out for number one that they are constantly stepping in number two.

So, how do we make wise decisions? I suggest applying the problem solving approach, the arm wrestling technique, the Golden Rule of do unto others as you would have others do unto you and all the other tools and guidelines in this book. Try them. If they work for you, keep them and make them yours. If they do not work then throw them away, but never stop searching for better approaches to making life work.

One key component of wise decision making is to base our decisions on the UniverSOUL principle that we are all one. As we see others, so are we ourselves. As we treat others, so do we treat ourselves. Who we are is so connected and blended with all others that it is literally impossible to not be doing to ourselves what we are doing to them. We are the spiritual embodiment of each other. We cannot, for example, confine them without confining ourselves. When we damage or hurt someone we damage or hurt ourselves. We cannot be truly free unless all are free. If even one person is not free then none of us are free. We cannot be truly loved unless all are loved. When we do not love someone we do not love ourselves. When we do not love a part of someone we do not love that part in ourselves. When we can open up our awareness far enough we will understand all people, all thoughts, all words and all behaviors. **The seeking of true freedom necessitates learning to see ourselves in all others and all others within ourselves.**

The Rings of Life

One way of operating from the UniverSOUL point of view is to take into account all the components of our lives. I call these THE RINGS OF LIFE and I visualize these as looking like a target. In the center is the bulls-eye. This bulls-eye is our self, the "I" or, more accurately, where the "I" is presently being centered. The second outer circle or ring would be the "We" and would be us with a mate, if we have one. The third ring, the "Us" would be our family unit and include children, ourselves, spouses, roommates, significant others and family members if they lived with us, if we have them. The fourth ring is an expression of our self in a larger context and would include our home, possessions, pets, property and all that is contained within its boundaries such as trees and plants. The fifth ring is our neighborhood. This includes the people, buildings, yards, parks, roads and sidewalks. The sixth ring is our city, town or village along with the inhabitants and all else that exists there including the water, land and air. The seventh ring is our county. The eighth ring is our state, province or territory. The ninth is our country. The tenth is our continent including the water and air surrounding it. The eleventh is our planet. The twelfth is our solar system. The thirteenth is our galaxy. The fourteenth is our universe including the UniverSOUL.

I view this target as three-dimensional. Imagine it as an inverted multi-layer wedding cake, which if looked at from underneath would look like a 14-ring bulls-eye. As we move beyond our self (the "I") we progressively enlarge the context of the expression of our self and who we are. The number of rings you have would vary of course, depending on the country you live in and how they label their geographical divisions. Also, your job would fit into these rings. It would be found on whatever level your job operates on. For example, if you run a small neighborhood grocery store that primarily serves the people in that area then your job would be part of your fifth ring. If you work for a national company that basically serves your country, then your job would be on the ninth ring.

Family members that are not living in the home such as parents, siblings, children, grandparents and other relatives would be a part of the ring in which they live that is in relation to your location. For example, if your parents lived in your state, but not in your county, they would be a part of your eighth ring. You could have family on many rings.

If we are looking to make wise choices in life, we should first find out how our decisions would impact on all the circles of who we are. We are much more than just an "I". We belong to all twelve circles. One way of measuring the UniverSOUL awareness of an individual is by assessing how many circles the being takes into account when making a decision.

Each of these circles or levels is a context in which we have an opportunity to experience our larger and higher self. They are opportunities to learn about, learn from and experience our self in a larger context and on a bigger scale. Unfortunately, we have been losing touch with our oneness with all people and things as a consequence of getting stuck in the "I". There are steps we can take if we wish to help develop these outer circles of who we are, once we are aware of their existence. This process can begin by taking time to meditate on and experience our self on each one of the rings or levels. Start with the "I" level and experience yourself expanding as you move your way through the rings. Experience each one as fully as possible using as many senses as possible. Do not *imagine* that you are there, but rather *be* there. Another way of experiencing or growing on all or most of the rings at once is to find a cause to promote that you believe in and that will help promote growth of who you are on those rings. For example, if you were to help an illiterate person to read that would be improving many, if not all of your levels. You will have made the world a better place.

Keep in mind that when you help this person to read that it is really yourself that you are helping on those levels. This is because that person you are helping *is* a part of you on those levels. For instance, there will be one more person in your county that can now read. Since you are part of that county (on the seventh ring), you as a county has now improved and grown. This is the method we need to employ to improve the world. We need to recognize that each one of those levels *is* us. What we do to them, we do to us. They are us.

Being Right Versus Making Things Go Right

The importance of considering our contexts or components is no less essential than that of considering our priorities. This was once again made readily apparent to me on a drive to work one day. Part of my drive used to require me traveling on a particular interstate highway. On one stretch of the road there is a sign that says slower traffic keep right. I was on this part of the road, in the fast lane, when I found myself gaining on the car in front of me. He didn't move over to the right, so I went around him. As I did I noticed that it wasn't one car in front of me, it was two. The driver that had been directly in front of me was riding right on the bumper of the car in front of him. (In case you were wondering, yes, they were both men.) I assume the message the man in car number two was trying to send to the lead car was to either pick up speed or move out of the way.

The man in car two was "right" the front car should have gotten out of his way. However, I was going faster than both of them and they both should have moved out of my way. Even if it wasn't the law, it is simple road courtesy. At any rate, I could see the man in car two was angry and probably the man in car one was also. It seemed that the man in car two felt a need to prove to the man in front of him, as well as to the other cars around him, that he was right and the driver in front of him was wrong and was a jerk.

As I went past the two cars and on down the highway I looked in my rearview mirror. I could see back on the horizon that car two was still riding on the rear bumper of the car in front of him. I imagined that the man in car two got into work late that morning. I could picture the boss being annoyed and asking why he was late. The man would answer with a half-truth saying that some jerk on the road was blocking his path and would not let him by. I see the boss now being irritated and taking it out on his secretary. The secretary becomes irritated and takes it out on a customer. The customer becomes upset and takes it out on his spouse when he gets home. The spouse takes her irritation out on her daughter who takes it out on her younger brother who then kicks the family dog. The dog looks perplexed and thinks, "What did I do? Boy, these humans are crazy." Crazy humans indeed.

Even if the whole scenario of the trickle-down emotional reaction by the boss did not occur, I could see that the man in car two was angry and may have gotten in to work late. Myself, I was at work on time and in a good mood.

The driver in car two and myself were both "right", the man in car one should have moved over. There is a difference, however, between the driver of car two and myself. He got stuck in trying to prove he is right. I chose to make things go right. I didn't have a need to prove to myself or anyone else that I was right. Therefore, I could let go of it. I didn't dump on myself. **We can choose a priority of being right or making things go right.**

Because of the ego and the belief systems we hold, we not only have difficulty accepting the idea of being wrong, but we have great insistence at "having" to be right. We want to believe and espouse the "fact" that we are right whether we are actually right or wrong about a given situation. We are afraid to be wrong. We would rather give up truth in order to feel that sense of rightness. We prefer a false sense of rightness than a true sense of wrongness. Every time we do this we lose the battle for awareness, growth and truth. As a well-known British band sang, we trade "a walk-on part in the war for a lead role in a cage." What good is it if a person exchanges a small part in a noble battle for truth, for a role of wealth or fame that costs him his true freedom? When we are wrong we feel threatened and can not deal with it. We want to perceive ourselves as being right and have developed many mind games we play on ourselves and others to "verify" that we are right. It is as if when we are right it is not enough for our self to *know* we are right. We feel a need to prove it to all those involved. **One is only free to the extent that one is truthful about, and to, one's**

self.

Again, when we catch ourselves stuck in the mind game or ego game of having to prove we are right we need to stop, evaluate and acknowledge our stuckness to ourselves and all that are within earshot. The truth shall set us free. As you become more open and express the real you (flaws and all), the more you make it okay for others to do the same.

We can help a person who is stuck in having to be right. The problem originates with their insecurity and lowered level of self-esteem. The way to help is to acknowledge their rightness in all the situations where that is the truth. Even when it is something so small you feel it is unimportant. When the individual begins to recognize how often that he is right he will feel more secure, his self-esteem will rise and he will feel much less of a need to prove he is right.

When we are all able to let go of having to prove we are right it enables us to come from a more UniverSOUL position of willingness to listen, consideration of all possible viewpoints, compassion for others and more able to make decisions based on the greatest good. If we do not, we pay the price. Parents who "have" to be right create children who "have" to be right.

Remember too, that the more frequent we are able to let go of having to be right the more often we are stretching and opening up to other viewpoints. Just as with physical exercise, the more we stretch the easier it is to attain greater growth and success that otherwise would have been out of our reach. As Supreme Court Justice Oliver Wendell Holmes stated, **"Man's mind stretched to a new idea never goes back to its original dimensions."**

Whether it is considering the validity of the ideas in this book or just living life in general, we need to be able to adjust and adapt our belief systems and our template, or view, of the world. In order to operate at optimum efficiency and effectiveness in the world we need to have our *beliefs of what is* match as closely as possible to *what actually is.* Put another way, our beliefs should simply try and match reality. We need to see life as it is. This is particularly true of problems. As mentioned earlier, if we do not see a problem accurately, then we can not adequately solve a problem.

It seems advisable, therefore, that we keep an objective and open mind in order to add to our understanding. If we attempt to interact with the world with the readily-rejecting, prejudged view of a cynic then we are likely, at times, to be discarding the truth. Conversely, this does not mean that we should accept all that we hear and read as being the truth. That would be foolish. The most advantageous approach would seem to be that of keeping a fluid or open mind toward life that allows us to assimilate and accommodate new information into our present-time operating system. There is, I suppose, nothing so terrible about being a skeptic, as long as we do not slip into cynicism. To me a cynical person is someone who is striking out at the world because of the pain they feel inside.

It seems that many people take strong stands on issues and as a result often consciously or subconsciously ignore or misinterpret further information. This may be called stubbornness, bias or bigotry. A person who has an open mind should be able to be receptive to, examine and integrate new information. There does seem to be a correlation between the breadth and range of our open mind and the spiritual heights that are achieved. It appears that the more latitude we have in our thinking the more altitude we can achieve as a spirit. The door seems to be unlocked by the keys of inclusion and acceptance.

American drama critic Brook Atkinson said, **"The most fatal illusion is the settled point of view. Since life is growth and motion, a fixed point of view kills anybody that has one."** It is the abandonment of a fixed point of view that brings about change and growth spurts. By getting off our fixed position and stretching, and not having the need to be right, we create new possibilities. Notice that I am not saying do not hold a point of view. When we hold an open point of view we are able to accommodate and assimilate new information. Everything in this universe is in a constant state of flux. Everything is constantly moving and changing. Nothing remains stable. What appears to remain stable is an illusion. The table or chair near you appears unmoving, but it is just that. It *appears* unmoving. Actually, it is moving on two levels. On one level it is on this planet and the planet is moving, therefore, they do not occupy the same space that they did even a few seconds ago. Secondly, the table and chair are made up of atoms and molecules that are in a constant state of movement. As human beings we are the same. We are in a constant state of change. Since nothing remains stable we have only two options. One is to contract and shrink and the other is to expand and grow. You get to choose.

The more we choose to let go of the fixed viewpoint, judgments and false beliefs the more we will see the world distortion-free. The more therefore, we are in the moment and not of the moment. The more we are in the world, but not of the world.

Blind Spots

At this point in our human history it would not seem to far off base to say that if we looked up 'human being' in a dictionary one should not be surprised to see it defined as a being who distorts its world. We distort the world; for example, when we see our achievements as due to our hard work, yet when others succeed we often attribute it to luck. We distort the world in many ways, as is discussed throughout this book. At other times we do not see what is there. Just as when we drive a car, there are places that we cannot see in our range of vision or even with the aid of mirrors. We call these *blind spots*.

Similarly, we have all seen these blind spots in others. We are able to see their selfishness, harshness, prejudice or cruelty even though they cannot. What is difficult, is seeing it within ourselves. As you were reading these words you probably nodded your head yes, but you most likely avoided thinking about whether you had any of these or similar characteristics. On the other hand, you might have thought about it for a second and immediately ruled out the possibility that you might have any of the negative traits. Or possibly you thought you might be that way sometimes, but it's very, very rare that you are. Buddha stated, "Dwelling on your brother's faults multiplies your own." The Bible spoke about pulling a splinter out of your brother's eye, but having a log in your own. It certainly seems well-advised to open ourselves to these words of wisdom. In addition, if we truly wish to become free, we can also create contexts where we are open and receptive to the observations and opinions of others. If we are to actually achieve the UniverSOUL with full awareness it seems imperative that we put our heart and soul into creating it. **A half-hearted attempt is a whole-hearted failure.**

One individual may view himself as being a fair-minded and understanding person. Another might think of herself as a person who doesn't have problems or issues with controlling her anger. You yourself may fall into one of these categories or you may have some other like-minded self-belief. One pivotal aspect of life for all of us is that, at some point, we are generally presented with a situation where we have to rethink whether our self-view is accurate. When the situation presents itself it may occur internally as a consequence of something we think, do, say or observe. It may also come externally as a result of something that someone else says or does to us. The point is that we find ourself at a fork in the road having to question some aspect of our behavior or self-image. We have to challenge some component of who we have been believing we are. It typically seems to come about as a confrontation of two diametrically opposite views. Usually one is more negative and the other is more positive.

There are three primary ways of resolving this contradiction. One is to accept both aspects as being components of who we are. The second is to deny and defend. The use of this second method contains no growth. We merely reject the concept of having that negative attribute and put up defenses for protection. We may also use justifications and offensive maneuvers, such as blaming others (or the world) for it and not taking responsibility. Sadly, when we blame others we deny ourself the opportunity to transform.

The third way of resolving the contradiction is to earnestly examine the truth in the situation and not lie to our self. This is the high road. This is the road of awareness and the path of insight and transcendence. It might be a rougher road and one that is more of a struggle and a challenge. However, as you continue down the higher road you will find that it gives you a vantage point that the lower road can not provide. You are better able to see and understand life and yourself.

In actuality, the third way of resolving the contradiction often begins by taking the first way of resolving it and accepting that we may have both attributes or traits within us. This third way has one additional step that the first way lacks. That is, that we then begin to ask ourselves questions like: "Is this who I am? Is this who I want to be? Does this trait help my life to function better? Would I want someone else to be this way or treat me this way?" This allows us the opportunity for change.

Choosing to take the lower road may *appear* to be our best choice because it often is the path of least resistance, and requires the least time and effort. We may pay dearly for that choice throughout our life though. In the long run it will cost us much in lost awareness, growth and freedom. Be aware that we can all deceive ourselves, and we need be on guard if we do not wish to pay that price.

One other thought on this. If we choose to take option one or option three (the growth path) it is vital that we be conscious of *how* we present it to ourselves so that we do not deny those positive aspects of who we are. For example, you might say to yourself, "I am a good person, but I am an angry person." By putting the "but" in there you are making a statement of opposition to the first statement. The second statement is then made to be "contrary" to the first. Therefore, in a sense, you are saying that you are not a good person. It invalidates the goodness of who we are. How do we resolve this and yet still speak the truth? We use the word "and" instead of the word "but." For instance, "I am a good person *and* I am an angry person" or "I am a good person *and* I often get angry." Although this may seem to be wordplay, it is not. It allows us to make a more truthful statement without invalidating its positive and opposite attribute.

When life events present you with these contradictions see them for what they really are. They are doors to insight and awareness. Please do yourself a favor and take advantage of the opportunity. Use them. They can become revelations if you fully see what is being revealed to you.

Determine who you are and decide who you want to be.

The Five Basic Creation Points of Intention

A moment ago I spoke about the path of least resistance. Here is a technique to help understand resistance. I want you to try a little exercise. Take the palm of your open right hand and place it at face level in a vertical position with the fingers pointing up. Have the palm facing left so that your thumb is closest to you. Place it directly in front of your face about six inches from your nose. Now imagine that this hand is your intention. Your goal is to move your palm from the front of your face to a distance of about one foot to the left of your face. So, go ahead now and carry out that intention. Please, actually do the steps as you read these words in order to get the full effect. You finished it? Okay, good.

Now I want you to take your right palm and put it in the starting position again. This time take your left palm and place it against your right palm. They should look as if they are in a praying position. Now create an intention (but don't carry it out yet) to move your hand to the end position one foot to the left of your face at the same speed you previously moved it at. Before you begin carrying out the intention I want you to use a counter-force with your left hand that moves in the opposite direction. Do not make the counter-force of the left hand as powerful as the intention, force and speed of the right hand. I want you to use the amount of force with your left hand that it takes to slow the speed of your intention hand by half. This creates a resistance or counter-intention to your intention. So, go ahead and carry it out now. If done correctly it should have looked like the previous movement, but at half the speed. Good.

Now take both hands again and place them palm to palm in the starting position. This time I want you to use an equal amount of force with both hands. Now carry out that intention. Your hands should not be moving, but much energy and force is being expended. Good. Now double the force with both hands. Now double it again. Notice how much energy and force is being used, but that you make no forward progress with your intention. You get nowhere, yet you put out all this effort. Tiring, isn't it? And what a struggle.

Now place your hands in the starting position palm to palm. This time I want your counter-intention left hand to be twice as strong and as fast as your intention right hand. Begin. If done correctly your right hand should have been resisting at half the force of the left hand, so that your right hand was slowly being pushed about one foot to the right of your head. Good.

For the last step, place your left counter-intention hand in the starting position. Now move your left hand, unopposed, to a position about one foot to the right of your head. Excellent.

These are *The Five Basic Creation Points of Intention*. The first one is pure intention and is carried out without resistance or counter-intention. It allows a person or group to achieve their goals as quickly and efficiently as possible.

The second creation point is a mixture. You are able to accomplish your goal; however, you produce a struggle for yourself and waste a lot of energy and time by also creating counter-intention. You want to get an "A" on the exam, but you watch a movie or TV instead of studying. You are working against your own goal (intention) with your own counter-intention. It is self-sabotaging.

The third creation point is when you produce a balance between your intention and counter-intention. This one is exhausting. It's struggle, struggle, struggle. You expend the time, energy and effort, but remain at a standstill. It's a stalemate. You want to be rich, so you go out and earn money, but you gamble it away. Odds are (pun intended) that you will never achieve your goal.

The fourth creation point is one step forward and two steps back. You create a situation where you keep losing ground. You create a counter-intention that is stronger than your intention. You want to lose weight on a diet, but you keep cheating on the diet and actually keep increasing your weight. This is self-defeating intention. This is like saying that you want to go east and you keep getting on a bus that is going west. Another example would be a person who creates an intention to quit smoking. But because of the addiction and the pleasure-seeking counter-intention you not only continue to smoke, but to smoke even more. We can see this pattern change in some cases if more force or energy is introduced and added to the original intention. A medical doctor tells you, for example, that if you do not stop smoking now you will be dead within a year or two. This can help create an intention strong enough to overcome your counter-intention.

The fifth creation point is pure counter-intention. To be more precise it would be "nearly" pure counter-intention. It cannot be 100% pure because you cannot have a counter-intention without an intention. It would have nothing to be "counter" to. From this creation point we may have a thought about something and instantaneously rule it out. For example, I have a thought that I'd like to own my own business, then I immediately think, "Yeah, right. That's impossible." That is as close as it ever gets to becoming reality. Strong counter-intention is like running in place. You put out lots of energy, but you get nowhere. When you create thoughts, words or actions (TWA) that go against your goals you bring into creation a force that works against you. You become your own worst enemy, or as the old comic strip character Pogo stated, "We have met the enemy and he is…us."

What is really troublesome about counter-intention is that it is helping to create situations and realities that we say we do not want. This is especially problematic when the counter-intentions are being created by our self in a subconscious or semi-conscious state as a consequence of basically being unaware that we are creating the reality around us. We then tend to think that it is the world in general or certain people in particular that are *doing it to us.*

If we looked at intention as a thought, then counter-intention could be described as the thought opposing the thought or, at times, it is the thought behind the thought. It explains why we sometimes fail in our attempts to create the reality, goal or life that we wish. **Counter-intentions gain reality-creating power to the degree that we possess counter-thoughts, counter-words and counter-actions on that particular factor.**

We could describe intention as the willful thought or plan that leads to the act of moving in the direction of a particular goal. In order to achieve our goals and create the realities that we want in this world, the most effective creation point we can come from is intention without counter-intention. **Pure intention creates instantaneously.**

The fact that we have the obstacles of defense mechanisms and triggers associated with our past history to overcome, creates counter-intention and increases the difficulty in achieving our goals. They hinder the creative process and make goals tougher to attain without effort and struggle. Having said this, I must add that the degree of difficulty and struggle is based on the extent to which the beliefs in these two sentences have dominion over your belief system.

Howard Taylor went so far as to say this about the power of our beliefs: **"Whatever the mind of man can conceive and believe he can achieve."**

For those of us who find ourselves unable at present to always come from pure intention there is a gradient scale of procedures we can use. If we examine the chance of something occurring we can rank it into three degrees of likelihood. They are possible, probable and absolute. Similarly, as Neale Donald Walsch described, there are three levels of belief, which I call the Three Levels of Confidence. They are hope, belief and knowing. Hope is a feeling or wish that what is wanted will happen or be received. The second level is belief. Belief is accepting something as true even though absolute certainty may be absent. Belief involves faith and trust. The Bible says that if we have the faith of a mustard seed that we shall move mountains. The third and highest level is to know. Knowing means to be sure and certain of something. It contains no doubt. Attached to hope and belief is some degree of doubt or fear. It is a fear that the something might or might not happen. It is that fear that keeps hope and belief from becoming knowing. Knowing contains no fear. **Only fear keeps you from knowing.**

If we take our levels of hope belief and knowing and apply them to our thoughts, words and actions we then have a way of increasing the effectiveness of our abilities in the creative process. If we create a knowing in our choice of thoughts, a knowing in our choice of words and a knowing in our choice of actions then we have created the absolute optimum environment for the germination of our creation. **Making optimum choices tends to bring optimum results.**

Optimum comes from the same root word as optimism. Optimism is the tendency to assume a point of view that expects the best outcome in any situation. Pessimists tend to expect misfortune and the worst possible outcome in any circumstance. They perceive everything as a problem and every problem as permanent and leading to disaster and catastrophe. Optimists perceive upsets, obstacles and setbacks as being temporary challenges and know that since they are temporary that they can be overcome or transcended. It's the age-old question of whether the cup is half-full or half-empty. Much, if not all, of life is a matter of interpretation and the way we perceive it does influence what follows. The ability to not turn setbacks into catastrophes creates a resilience to life's upsets. Similarly, I believe that approaching life from a spiritual point of view gives us a spontaneous buoyancy and an ability to nimbly rebound when we encounter setbacks. I expect we will see much more information coming out about the subject of optimism in the near future and the power that it contains for us as spiritual beings. Optimism can benefit our mental, emotional and physical health and thereby, improve the quality of our lives. It can also assist in transcending failure and breeding success.

It has been said that 95% of all obstacles are perceived. No one has described this
mental mirage better than Grant Frazier when he stated that, "**Life is full of obstacle illusions.**" It is truly an illusion when we perceive an obstacle as insurmountable and unable to be overcome or conquered. When we do we are limiting ourselves in the worst way. We are bringing about our own defeat.

Spiritual beings on the UniverSOUL level have no limitations. They are limitless. The limitations and restrictions we experience, even as a spirit operating a body, are all self-imposed limitations.

One reason our self-defeating and negative thoughts are so powerful is because they often result in, or become, a negative action unless stopped. It is precisely this "sinking thinking" that keeps us down and prevents us from rising up to the heights of our true selves. I believe that if we examined our self-defeating choices we would find a foundation that was built out of irrational fears.

The wonderful thing about this connection between our thoughts and actions is that the same applies for positive thoughts. If we do not stop a positive thought it will generally become a positive action with positive consequences. See the beauty, the love, the truth, the rightness and the positiveness in all that is around you and allow this to be foremost in your thoughts. **Flooding your mind with positive thoughts leads to positive actions that result in positive consequences.**

The Incredible Power of Attention

We can create this positive state of mind. American philosopher and psychologist William James declared a century ago that the greatest revolution of his generation was the discovery that human beings can change the outer aspects of their lives by changing the inner attitudes of their minds. To achieve this we need to become more conscious of what we think about and then choose whether or not it furthers our life purpose to think about that particular thought. This process begins with our attention. Our attention is the seed that develops into the thoughts, words and actions that create our reality. Where and how we focus our attention determines what we experience and how we feel. Look what happens, for example, if we focus too much attention too often on the future. When we dwell on it we tend to get anxious, nervous and worried. Notice that all these reactions are fear-based. When we focus too much attention for too long on the past we tend to feel sad or depressed and may experience guilt or regret. It can also create anger. That is because anger and depression are two sides of the same coin. Sigmund Freud, the psychoanalyst, pointed out that depression is anger turned inward, that is, anger that is unexpressed and kept inside us will often turn into depression. So, when we focus too much attention on our past, anger and depression are frequently experienced. **Life is not what was, nor is it what will be. Life is what is now.**

Similarly, what we do with our attention in present time greatly impacts on us. It has been said that when a pickpocket walks down the street all he sees are people's pockets. This is because he focuses his attention there. Most people walking down a street would probably not even notice people's pockets. Imagine yourself walking down the street. What do you focus your attention on? The attractive person walking by? The cars going down the street? The trees or flowers? The clothes people are wearing? Details about the buildings? Hairstyles? Noise levels? There is an interaction that takes place between our attention and our thoughts. At times, our attention brings about our thoughts and at other times our thoughts bring about our attention.

Where and what you focus your attention on says as much about you as the beliefs or interpretations you have about what it is that you are perceiving. Think of how much you could learn about yourself if you were able to spend just one day monitoring what you focus your attention on. As you walk through your life make an attempt to become more aware of what your attention is cast upon. Then look for patterns and evaluate what that may be saying about you. And what are the consequences of spending your attention there. Then choose whether or not you want to continue focusing your attention on those things, but base your decision on whether that reflects either who you are or who you want to be. Poet Ralph Waldo Emerson wrote, "What lies behind us and what lies before us are tiny matters to what lies within us."

The Principles of Attraction

There seems to be a principle of attraction that begins with attention and results in an attraction reaction. **The Principles of Attraction are: First, by focusing our attention on someone or something, it causes that someone or something to become more real, solid and detailed. Second, as someone or something becomes more real, solid, and detailed, we make judgments and interpretations about it. Third, by making our judgments or interpretations on that someone or something, it causes us to resist or desire the person or thing. Fourth, by experiencing resistance to, or desire for, a person or thing it causes it to persist and be drawn toward us.**

When we look at or feel something we are giving it our attention. When we give something our attention we endow it with energy and life. We often do this in regard to fear, which then brings about the very thing that we fear. Researchers have gathered scientific evidence in recent years about how the observer affects that which is observed. By the apparent simple act of observing we are influencing what we are looking at. This is the process by which we bring positives and negatives into our life. Therefore, it seems obvious that we be conscious of where we place our focus, and that it be on what we want to create rather than on what it is we fear. **Use your attention to allow your dreams, rather than your fears, to become the seed of the reality you create.**

Reality is the state or quality of being real and true rather than illusory. We can impact on this reality by how and where we focus our attention.

The more we focus our attention on something the more real it can become. Three factors of attention that help determine that reality are frequency, duration and intensity. Frequency is how often we focus on or think about the item or event. Duration is how long in each instance or situation we focus on the item or event. Intensity is the degree of concentration we bring to focus on the item or event.

To get some idea how much power our attention has in shaping our reality consider the following information. Our senses process about eleven million bits of data per second. Our consciousness, however, processes only about 16 bits of data per second. So, where we focus our attention greatly determines what and how we perceive, and consequently, how we interpret our world. Toward this endeavor of harnessing our attention we do seem to have one thing in our favor. Our species has one advantage that appears to be unique. Among all species we alone seem to have the ability to change our perceptions, our interpretations and our expectations and therefore, the ability to transform our reality.

In order to manifest what you want in this physical world you need to apply several principles. Before you start, be sure to place your focus on the ends, not on the means. In other words, if it is a desire for money then do not focus on money, but rather focus on what it is that you want the money to provide you with. First, determine what the desire or intention is. Second, let go of any counter-TWA or any counter-beliefs you may have. If you do not rid yourself of the counter-intention you will be working against your own goals. Third, use your imagination and faith and visualize it in your mind as if you have already achieved or acquired what you desire. Pour your feelings into this desire. Seeing it and feeling it brings it into reality. So, use all of your senses to begin creating it in your mind. See it, hear it, feel it, taste it and touch it. Do this on a very in-depth and detailed level. Then come from a place of absolute expectation without limits. You need to believe that failure is impossible. Have total and complete faith and expectation. Fourth, fully apply your thoughts, words and actions toward the manifestation of your creation. Remember that there are three levels of confidence (i.e., hope, belief and knowing) that you can apply to your thoughts, words and actions. Knowing is the highest level. It is absolute. So have a knowing that you have manifested your creation.

Creating what you want in life is not as difficult as some may believe. If you believe however, that it is difficult or impossible, then that is what you will create. Let's approach this from a positive viewpoint and say that it is an object (i.e., money or a job) that a person wants. That object is in the hands of someone else. Remember that we are supposed to act and behave as if we already have it. The person who has the money, when viewed from the physical STEM world is separate from us, but viewed from the spiritual world is connected to us. It is similar to berber carpeting. Each loop of the carpet looks individual, but when you look deeper than the outward appearance you see that each loop is connected to the other loops. If you pull on one loop it unravels other loops because beneath the surface they are connected. It is like the loose thread on a knit sweater. If you begin to pull on it you will find that it is all connected. Since we (human beings) are all one then that person who has the item or the money now (on one level) is you. Therefore, you already have the money, item, job, condition, etc. You just need to fully realize it. The reason those on higher levels of awareness find it easier to create their realities is because as they become more and more aware of the fact that we are one with all others it helps in the manifestation of their creations by realizing, in a sense, that they truly do already have it.

Recognize that the other person is generally willing to give up whatever it is that you want. If you think about it you will see that all of us give up money (by spending it), give up homes (by moving), give up jobs (by quitting or getting a new job) and so on. When this occurs we are exchanging these things from one person to another.

Think of how to approach it. If it is a job you want then visualize the creation of a new job coming to the person who's position you will take. Imagine them getting a promotion or a better job offer and it results in you getting their old position. The religious leader Mohammed said, "Wish for others whatever you wish for yourself." Do not just focus on what you want. Find a way to also give it away or help obtain it for someone else. When you do, it proves to yourself, your mind, and your universe that there is an abundance of whatever it is that you want. Your mind and yourself will come to believe that there must be an abundance or you would not be trying to give it away. So, put your energies in such a direction and it will come back to you. Then, focus on knowing that you have already received it. React as you would react if this happened. Allow yourself to fully feel that experience. Be thankful and grateful. Get excited! Be thrilled! Similarly, even the New International Version of the Bible (Mark 11:24) advocates, "Therefore I tell you, whatever you ask for in prayer, believe that you have received it, and it will be yours."

Once you have created and experienced these images then let go of the need to have the desired result occur. In other words detach yourself from the outcome you desire. Just allow it to be. Let go and have faith. Your focus should be on the process rather than on the result. Faith comes from knowing that everything is happening for a reason and that regardless of how it may seem, that reason is loving, compassionate and good. We can obtain peace. We can be happy. We can acquire awareness. We can manifest our creations. The manifestation of all these things can be further aided by not only having the point of view of acceptance of that which is, but *choosing* that which is. So, do not let go of the intention, just let go and discard the *need* to have that particular result. This is because if you still have the need then you do not have what it is that you want and you are supposed to be behaving with faith and knowing that you already have it.

If you question the above use of imagination (i.e., imagining that you already have the item) or say that it is just imagining and therefore, that it is not real then keep in mind that creation occurs with the use of imagination and faith. Imagination without the use of faith is just pretending. Be clear on this and do not confuse imagining with pretending.

People often become frustrated because what they create or what they plan appears not to come to fruition. They may plan, for example, that they are going to go out to the dance tonight and have an expectation of meeting a potential mate. They go and end up not getting the immediate results they want in the place they expect. They then think they have failed, that they are not worthy or they feel that they are unable to create what they wish for. In actuality, it just is not true. It is just that it comes from another place and/or another time. Our creations are not always immediately fulfilled. You might do a good turn here, but it comes back to you there. Sometimes, before the creation has arrived, an individual creates counter-intention to his own creation, which then prevents it from being attained. An example of this is, "I don't know why I bothered. I won't get the job anyway", or "They didn't call, so someone else must have gotten the job" or "Well, I really didn't want the job anyway." Just because the package did not arrive when you thought it should does not mean that it is not in the mail.

In recent years researchers have done work at the sub-atomic level that has indicated that the observer appears to affect that which is observed. This implies that by simply observing an event we may have power or influence over that event. This is a bombshell and a breakthrough revelation. Whether the thoughts, intentions or expectations of the observer cause this influence or whether it is their mere presence is a question I would be excited to know the answer to. The ramifications of this research are far-reaching, especially in regard to our ability to create reality and manifest our desires and creations.

Approach and Retreat

As stated earlier in step four of The Principles of Attraction when we resist or desire something it causes that person, object or situation to be drawn toward us. We are very aware of the fact that if we desire something we can try to reach out and obtain it. It does not matter if it is a glass of water, a pencil, a job or a relationship. This is the typical way we draw something to us. We approach it or advance toward it. This is not the only way however. The other way is to resist it or withdraw from it. I call this mechanism **Approach and Retreat**. If you try one method and it does not work you may want to try the other. I have had numerous couples over the years that have come in to my practice for 'couple counseling' as a result of this mechanism. A common scenario is where the wife is unhappy in the marriage and asks her husband countless times (the approach) to go into marital therapy with her. He repeatedly refuses. Finally she packs her bags, is standing at the front door and tells him goodbye and exits (the retreat). He chases after her (the approach) and they end up in therapy. Keep in mind that an approach (or retreat) can be expressed in our thoughts, words or actions.

Another scenario is when someone is trying to sell something (the approach) to another person. At some time the potential buyer feels that the seller is being a high-pressure salesman and backs away (the retreat). If the seller does not realize what he is doing he will most likely lose the sale. If he does realize, it would serve him well to stop the high-pressure tactics and back off. He might then make the sale.

I have actually applied this technique to little children. You can try and reach out for them, but they run and hide behind their mother. Instead, I look at them and then quickly look away. I do this several times. When they start looking back at me I shield my eyes and turn my head. Soon I'm peeking out from behind my hands and they are coming closer. Soon I'm completely turning my body away from them and they are running up trying to see under my hands. Before I know it they are climbing up in my lap and trying to pull my hands away from my eyes.

Some may call this manipulation. I don't. As with all mechanisms, rules and laws of life I believe it has to do with the intention and purpose that is behind the action. The husband spoken about earlier, for example, was unaware of the extent of his wife's dissatisfaction with their relationship. Not that I am putting the blame on her, it's just that her efforts were not enough to awaken him (too little effort with her arm wrestling). So when she took the action to withdraw, he realized what it would be like to lose her and saw that it was not what he wanted.

In many ways the effectiveness of this withdrawal action is similar to the magnetic effects in a bar magnet. If you reach for something and it seems to pull away then you may be repelling it because you are coming at something from a different direction (i.e., your north poles are facing each other and are therefore pointing in different directions). So what you might need to do is reverse yourself and instead of reaching, turn around and go in the opposite direction from the other person. That is, that both of your north poles would now be facing in the same direction. In magnetism "opposites attract." Thus, when you head away from him with your north pole, your south pole will be facing his direction. This would attract his north pole to your south pole. I believe the reason this occurs is because it creates an alignment rather than a resistance. When the north pole of one bar magnet attaches to the south pole of another bar magnet, they are in alignment and act as if they are one magnet. There becomes only one north pole and one south pole when they are joined.

Scarcity Versus Abundance

It also ties in with scarcity versus abundance. The reason most people would rather have a handful of diamonds than a handful of dirt is because of their value. The diamonds are considered to be more valuable than a handful of dirt because of their scarcity. Food or water, for example, is considered to be more valuable in a country where it is scarce than in a country where there is an abundance. In general, when an artist dies his paintings tend to become more valuable because no more will be made. Thus, insuring a limited supply. If the demand for them is there, a scarcity will eventually occur. In a similar fashion, if a person makes their self too available, some people may take them for granted. This explains why a person, at times, may get used by others or does not get a date, a job or respect from other people. Others assume you will always be there whenever they need or want you. For some people to appreciate the value of someone or something it may be necessary to create a scarcity of it.

One other aspect to consider about attraction and attention is that focusing our attention on something can at times be an addiction, just as it can be with our thoughts, words and actions. This addiction can take us out of present time, can lead us away from who we really are, and can take away our freedom and choice. Clues to, or indications of, these addictions can be obtained in a number of ways. One, we may find ourselves focusing on someone or something that we wish we were not focusing on. Two, we may believe that someone or something is unhealthy for us to be focusing on. Three, we may try to justify reasons for focusing on someone or something. Four, we allow ourselves to be open to someone we trust to tell us about any unhealthy habits or patterns that they observe in us as blind spots.

How do we go about defeating these addictions and freeing ourselves? Ken Keyes, Jr., author of "Handbook to Higher Consciousness", suggests that we begin by turning our addictions into preferences. Instead of feeling that we must act on the addictive impulse we can begin to reduce the strength of the addiction by viewing it as a preference rather than an addiction. So, we say to ourselves that I do not have to act on that impulse I would just prefer to act on it. That way we open ourselves up to accepting and choosing other possibilities that are not our first preferences. This not only helps free us from the addictions we have, but typically reduces our negative emotion because we can more readily accept not getting a preference that we would have liked than we can accept not getting someone or something that we 'must' have.

The Limitations of Attention

Our attention does have limitations. This can vary in degree from person to person and from one time to another time. A more aware individual has more attention to use in present time. This is because they have worked through some of their past history and are, therefore, carrying around less excess baggage. First, they do not have as much attention locked up in their past and secondly, they are not expending as much energy keeping the subconscious demons down and out of their conscious mind. As a person grows more aware and conscious they free up more units of attention. The more aware individual also has less need for, and use of, defense mechanisms, which frees up additional units. They are more open to accepting reality as it is without feeling a need to defend themselves, avoid the reality or deny it. This confronting of reality reduces the loss of, and creates opportunities to increase the amount of, attention units. Thus, increasing our power to create.

People have varying amounts of attention available to them. If we measured this in dollars we could say that one person might only have \$1.00 worth of attention whereas another individual who is more aware may have \$5.00 worth. Whether a person has \$1.00 worth or \$5.00 worth it is still 100% of the present time attention available to them at that point in time. I use these figures as a way to explain attention to my patients. I will often do a little exercise to show them the extent and power of their attention.

I begin by saying to the patient that I am going to tell them something that is going to dramatically change their lives, but I will only tell it to them one time. If they miss it, it will be gone forever. I tell them I need 100% of their attention. I tell them that once I say the words to them that I will want them to repeat the words back to me in exactly the same way I say the words to them. Once I have their attention I raise a finger as if I am going to make a point and I begin to open my mouth, but I say nothing. I don't make an utterance for about ten seconds, or at least until I hear some external sound. It might be the air conditioning or heat turning on, music out in the waiting room, a phone ringing in another office, a clock ticking, or traffic noises outside. I then tell them, "I'm not going to say anything. I was just checking to see if I fully had your attention." I then pause if the sound is still occurring, I ask them to listen, and then ask them if they hear whatever sound I heard during the ten seconds. They typically say that they hear it now. If the sound is no longer there I will ask them if they heard the phone or the traffic, for example, or whatever I heard during the ten seconds. If they say no they didn't hear it when they were paying attention to me then I ask them how come they didn't hear it. They generally say they didn't hear it because they were giving me 100% of their attention. If they say they did hear it during the 10 seconds, then I say they didn't give me 100% of their attention because if they had they wouldn't have heard the sound. I remind them that it is similar to reading a book or being absorbed watching TV when a family member taps them on the shoulder and asks, "Didn't you hear me calling you. I was telling you that dinner was ready." The person was so engrossed in what they were doing that they did not hear the family member calling at all. Normally we walk through life a flashlight casting a wide beam with our attention. When we focus our full attention on one thing we become more powerful like a laser beam. This is also the basis on how hypnosis works.

In the second step of the exercise I ask them if they could imagine watching two young children in the room and not let them get into anything if I had to step out of the room for five minutes. They usually respond, "Yes." I then say, "Could you watch four kids for me?" They respond, "Sure." "How about eight kids" I ask. They answer, "Okay." Then I say, "How about sixteen or thirty-two?" They typically respond, "I don't think so." When I ask why, they say it's because they can't watch them all at once. It's too many. I say that's exactly right. You have to spread your attention so thin that it becomes ineffective.

I explain to the patient that the exercises have several purposes. One is a realization that we can bring things into our awareness by focusing on them and we can tune things out of our awareness by focusing our attention on something else. I should mention that I always make a point of teaching this to my chronic pain patients to help provide them with some level of control over their pain. They may not be able to make the pain go away, but they can gain some control by reducing their awareness of it. Some have been able to completely reduce their experience of the pain for periods of time. So, to a certain extent, they can sometimes feel pain-free. They can help achieve this by focusing 100% of their attention on other thoughts or tasks. There are four factors in those thoughts or tasks that appear to aid us in shifting our focus. They are carrying out a complex thought or task, carrying out a fine motor skill task that requires precision, carrying out multi-tasks at the same time and choosing tasks that we perceive as interesting and intriguing. The most effective is using some combination of the four of these.

The second purpose is to gain the realization that our attention has limitations and boundaries even though the boundaries can be expanded with increased awareness. If we have $1.00 worth of attention and spend all of the $1.00 then we have no attention left to spend on anything else. We have reached our limit. We may, of course, divide up the $1.00. We might spend forty cents focusing on this, twenty cents paying attention to that, twenty-five cents on this other and fifteen cents on that and thus, use up our $1.00.

The third purpose is the recognition of the incredible power that lies in our attention. We generally take it for granted and either basically perceive it as insignificant or simply do not think about it. Yet, it has great power and is the beginning process of drawing something to us. For this reason we should learn to control where we direct our attention. If we focus our attention on something we do not like or do not want, such as a fear, we can actually attract it and draw it to us. As we focus on it, it becomes more solid and real, that is, it can become reality. If we allow this to take place and operate with the subconscious mind in control we can create many events or experiences that we would prefer not to have. Similarly, we can bring into our lives many positive and joyous events by focusing our attention on them. The power that resides in our attention is clearly very under-appreciated and undervalued. The ability to create begins by the focusing of our attention.

In addition to choosing where to focus our attention it is also important to recognize the power that lies in focusing our attention on the here-and-now. In every activity we do we should try and be 100 percent in present time. We need to give precedence to focusing 100 percent of our attention to being in the moment. We should try and be aware of, and experience, every aspect of our existence in each and every present moment. In order to help us be more in present time we need to become conscious of our breathing and as much of the information coming in from our senses of taste, touch, smell, sight and sound as possible. Do not think about what is being experienced because that just activates the mind and puts the mind in control. Do not think – just experience. The idea is to be in the now and to disengage the mind.

Worry Versus Concern

Power lies in deciding *where* we choose to focus our attention and the difference in the results as a consequence of that choice can be very dramatic. Let us look at the experience of worry for example. Worry is all emotional. It is spinning your wheels and going nowhere. I often use an example of a person sitting on their front porch worrying about their dog going out into the street and getting hit by a car. The worrier just keeps saying to themselves, "I hope the dog doesn't get hit by a car. I hope the dog doesn't get hit by a car. I hope the dog doesn't get hit by a car." Worry not only does not help the situation; it usually makes things worse.

In my view we do not have to go down the path of worry. A better choice would be to take the path of concern. Where worry is all emotion, concern comes from thoughts and logic. I am not saying that there is no place for emotion. Emotion is one of the greatest gifts we have as human beings. I am saying that in many situations emotions such as worry do not help us and, in fact, they often worsen the situation.

When I think of the word 'concern' I always attach another word to it. That is the word 'do'. If we are concerned about something, we 'do' something about it. We take action (which is, if you remember, one of the steps of creating a new reality).

When we focus our attention on worry the situation does not improve and it often deteriorates further. When we focus our attention on concern and on doing we suddenly begin to come up with solutions. We can keep the dog in the house, we can put up a fence, put him on a leash, take him to obedience school, move out to the country, give the dog away, ask neighbors to watch out for him, petition the city to reduce the street speed limit, etc. We then draw these solutions to us. This is simply the process of applying the problem solving technique and TWA to the situation. When the issue is worry versus concern keep in mind that worry is destructive and concern is constructive. The only purpose I have found for worry is that it can serve as a signal to shift us into concern. **When worry shows up, concern should show it the door. The house of concern is the house of doing.** The next time a problematic situation arises for you imagine that you are standing at a fork in the road. One route is Worry Road. You look down it and you see gray, overcast skies; desolation; trash-littered streets; cracked sidewalks, bare trees; broken fences; paint peeling on dilapidated houses and vicious dogs growling in the background. Worry Road is a dead end street. The other route is Concern Avenue. When you look down this street you see smiling, friendly people; sunny skies; beautiful homes with well-kept yards; butterflies floating by; colorful flowers and plants; perfect humidity and temperature; and birds singing their melodious messages in the background. You get to choose which road you take. If without thinking, however, you suddenly find yourself on Worry Road, just take a side road over to Concern Avenue as quickly as possible. When the issue is worry versus concern keep in mind that worry is destructive and concern is constructive.

Once we have done all we can do to create the outcome we want to occur or have done all we can do to remedy or prevent a situation, then it is out of our hands. We need to let go of it. We can ask friends, family and specialists for any suggestions, but then there is nothing else we can do. The rest is in God's hands. If there is more you can do, then do it. If not, let it go. We either have control of a situation or we do not, so free your mind from worry and free your heart from fear. It serves no purpose to worry over something that we have no control over. This approach aligns itself perfectly with the Serenity Prayer: "God grant me the serenity to accept the things I cannot change, the courage to change the things I can and the wisdom to know the difference."

When we are going through difficult times we need to remind ourselves that "and this too shall pass" and it will. It always does. It's the nature of the universe. Even though we may not be able to see the light at the end of the tunnel, we can certainly *know* that the light is there.

The Boomerang Effect

I view humans as gardeners. This is certainly not a new concept. It has been passed down through the ages. We have all heard or read the words, "You reap what you sow" and, "What you plant is what you grow." Others are: "Output equals input" and "As you give, so shall you receive." It all works on the same basis as, "What goes around comes around." It has one basis in the eastern concept of karma. Karma is basically a moral law of cause and effect and is the view that the sum of our actions have consequences that determine our destiny. Therefore, what happens in our lives is a consequence of what we do. Every time we send out into the world a thought, word or action a similar response is sent back to us. This *Boomerang Effect* gives back to you whatever you are giving away. Imagine standing perfectly still in a pool of motionless water and throwing a rock into the water about eight feet away from you. Those ripples that come back and hit you are a result of what you send out into the world. Recognize also that the size of the rock is a major determiner of how big the waves are that hit you. Which is why when we are in a bad mood nothing seems to go right. In a sense, for every thought, word or action there is an equal and opposite thought, word or action. By opposite I do not mean that if we send out hate we get back love. What I mean is that if you send an energy or force out from yourself then an energy or force from the opposite direction comes back to you. So if we send out angry feelings then equal angry feelings will echo back to us from the opposite direction. What we intend for others comes back upon us. The solution is to live by the Golden Rule. **Do unto others, as you would have others do unto you.** Think for a minute on how many negative thoughts, words and actions you send out. Try for one day and become conscious of just how many you send out. Then choose to change the way you live in the world.

What You Seed Is What You Get

We are the gardeners of our life. As such, paying more attention to what we are planting can only benefit us. The job requires that we all become conscious, deliberate gardeners. As we plant our seeds we need to keep in mind that seeds can have different periods of germination and varying lengths of time until harvest. Try not to become pessimistic if the wait is longer than you anticipated. Most important though is that we recognize that if we plant hatred we grow hatred in our lives. If we plant anger toward others we grow anger toward ourselves. If we plant love, respect, compassion and sensitivity we get love, respect compassion and sensitivity. We cannot plant cucumber seeds and expect to get tomatoes. To rework an old phrase...**What you seed is what you get.**

If you are harvesting negatives then it seems logical that you planted them at some time. First, ask yourself, "What am I experiencing in my life that I don't want to be experiencing?" or "What negatives are occurring in my life that I don't want?" Then ask yourself, "What am I doing, or have I done, to create this unwanted situation or emotion?" Remember, it does not have to be something you just did. It could have even come out of a past life. Be careful though that you do not use a supposed past life cause as a way to avoid looking at the present or more recent past for the cause. In addition, if there are negatives they could also have been created by negative thoughts, such as a negative self-fulfilling prophecy, or negative counter-intention.

We need to ask ourselves, what seeds have we been planting today? What seeds are we planting as a couple, a family, a neighborhood, a community, a town or city, a state or province, a country, a continent and a planet? What seeds have we been planting as a culture, a religion or spiritual group, a class, a school, a business, a parent or child, a friend, a sibling, a club, an organization, a coworker, a stranger? I believe that if each one of us stopped planting the negative seeds and began planting the loving, positive ones that we would quickly achieve the unity and oneness that we all wish for our children and ourselves. We could achieve a union of the UniverSOUL.

Many individuals have been gardening for years and we have had many gardeners throughout the centuries, but now the time has come for all of us, like the caterpillar transforming into the butterfly. We know what to do; we just need to do it. It is so simple. Yet as human beings we apparently find it so hard to believe. Decide what it is you want and start giving it away, because it will come back to you even greater. You want love in the world? You know what to do.

It seems that we all have the responsibility to become good gardeners and plant the seeds of love, no matter how barren or tough the soil may be. I believe that there are now enough of us to bring about the change.

Mankind's Quantum Leap

I could say it no better than Paul Williams in his book Das Energi. He wrote, **"We are on the verge of a new age, a whole new world. Mankind's consciousness, our mutual awareness is going to make a quantum leap. Everything will change. You will never be the same. All this will happen just as soon as you're ready."**

I believe that we are in the midst of the greatest shift that has ever taken place on this planet. For centuries, and especially within the past half century, humankind has been on an internal spiritual quest. The journey in the last fifty years has been moving along at an incredible rate. I believe that the seeking and searching that has been going on internally is now going to be shared and experienced externally at levels and at a speed that will seem amazing. I would not be surprised to see the internet play a significant role in this also. I believe that we are on the cusp of seeing the spiritual implosion become a spiritual explosion. So, be alert. Be aware. You will begin to notice signs of the change coming.

With each person that works to raise the level of their own awareness and expressions of love it will spread and increase exponentially. It will serve as a catalyst for others that will assist them in manifesting their love and awareness. It has been said that, **"A rising tide raises all boats."** It seems that it is our fate that we strive to raise the collective consciousness.

The number of people who want to create a better, safer world is going to increase to the point of where a critical mass will be achieved. When this occurs the shift will take place. James Redfield, in his book, "The Celestine Prophecy," predicted a spiritual, cultural transformation that would begin with a critical mass being reached. Deepak Chopra proposed, "The more people who are intent upon - or directing their conscious toward - a specific outcome, the more powerful and far-reaching the potential effect of that intention."

In a similar way, I believe that we are going to see and experience greater unity in all aspects of life. Previously opposing forces and those with opposing beliefs will begin to recognize the connectedness and oneness with their so-called opposite. Imagine this with science versus religion/ spirituality. I expect the process would tend to look something like this: religion/spirituality came about and presented its thesis. Then science was presented as an alternative viewpoint, an anti-thesis. If both continue to grow and become more aware I believe they will begin to see the truth that is present and similar in both of their viewpoints. When this occurs you will see a convergence and a union. We will have thesis, antithesis and finally synthesis. I believe that we will see this process occur in almost every area of life. As more and more people become aware of their spiritual nature, it will become more publicly accepted. This will result in a merging and a union of the spiritual worlds.

As our sense of oneness with all others begins to appear to us, our experiences of sadness, fear and suffering will reduce or disappear. This is because compassion and understanding create connection and awareness that dissipates anger and negative emotion.

As a child we begin to create a mental image of who we think we are. This is based on experiences, impressions, beliefs and feedback that we mostly get from our family, friends, enemies, teachers and neighbors. We also get a large dose of input from larger social groups and environmental influences such as our community, culture, religion, schools and society. This becomes our ego, our false self, which we then carry into life and try to protect from harm. It not only does not serve us well, it raids our spiritual bank of all the truth, freedom and awareness that it can carry away.

As we attempt to create our life through growth and awareness it needs to be very clear to us that we are also not our vacillating emotions and melodramatic scenes. An emotion is just an intensified physical experience of a matching thought. We are not our physical body. Nor are we our mind with its incessant discourses on everything under the sun (and beyond).

We are a unique spiritual being that is linked to all other spiritual beings. We are interconnected with all that *is* on a universal spiritual level.

Our life is a script that we are writing. We can decide what we want to put into the rest of the chapters that make up our lives. We can create the world we want. For some of us this lifetime is perhaps one-quarter, one half or three-quarters done. That means we have three-quarters, one half or one-quarter left to use. How do you choose to use it? We cannot change the past. We can change the present and the future. We should never allow fear to prevent us from doing what is right or keep us from creating our dreams. As is said in an ancient proverb that in later years is most often attributed to Benjamin Franklin, **"God helps those who help themselves."** I believe that once we initiate the action that God will be there to provide support. We want a better world, but have we, as individuals, done all we can to create that world. Why should I expect God to be willing to do for me what I am unwilling to do for myself?

Think Twice and Speak Once

We need to begin the process. We cannot let fear rule us. Success requires that we make wise choices. There is so much to learn and to do that *where* we begin does not matter as much as *that* we begin. One place to begin is to consider what we say and do. The problem is that it is typically easier, or at least more ingrained and programmed, to react than it is to think. If you find yourself blurting things out you may need to think more before you speak. One way I have found that helps to deal with this is based on an experience I had with an old carpenter. He told me about an old carpenter's rule of thumb to prevent mistakes. The rule is measure twice and cut once. I have taken liberties with the phrase. In therapy and in my own life I have changed it to, **"Think twice and speak once"** and **"Think twice and act once."** This has proven very useful and saved me from bad choices at times. It is like putting a second filter on the line, so that less of what you do not want to get out actually get out. Recognize that just because you have a thought or an urge does not mean that you have to act on it. A similar phrase was uttered by that worldly old western sage, Festus, of the TV show Gunsmoke. He said, as I remember, "God gave you two ears and one mouth, so you do a heap more listenin' than you do talkin'."

Everything that we say and do impacts on our lives and the lives of those around us, as well. Everything we say and do teaches people around us. It teaches them about us and about how life is. This is especially true of our children. In their early formative years and throughout their adolescent and teenage years they learn and absorb. Unfortunately, too often as adults we say one thing and do another. "We're a walking contradiction, partly truth and partly fiction" according to songwriter Kris Kristofferson. We contradict ourselves continuously because while we perceive our self to be a loving, caring, compassionate human being our thoughts, words and actions are routinely not pro-survival for our self, much less our species or any other species. Not only do we often not do what we say and think, but we often go in completely the opposite direction. We have embarked on a journey and seem to have chosen not to use our spiritual compass. It would be wise to look at these contradictions and how they impact on us. A good place to begin is to recognize and accept these contradictions within ourselves. To be all-encompassing and all-embracing and then explore and examine those apparent inconsistencies.

We have the ability to become more aware and more conscious of all that we say and do. Let's face it, we are all teachers. Even though we may not think about it, or rarely think about it, we are teachers in our homes, our workplaces, our social lives and with all of life. It is important to recognize this and attempt to live in a more conscious way because we do significantly impact on those around us. Back a hundred years ago Henry Adams reflected that, "A teacher affects eternity; he can never tell where his influence stops." What a powerful and thought-provoking statement. If we really think about this quote we can see the power that our words and actions are having. What we say and do today may easily echo for generations, centuries and possibly for all of time. So, it seems the question we should be asking ourselves is are we teaching the things that we can feel proud to teach. Or are we teaching anger, hate, bigotry, prejudice, racism, sexism, ageism, egotism, superstition, and bias? It begs the question, why do we not create heaven on earth instead? I believe the answer is simply "fear". Whatever reason we may give for why we do not focus on creating heaven on Earth, if we look further beneath the surface of that reason we will find a core based on fear.

It seems essential that we eradicate this type of fear from within ourselves on all levels. Fear creates separateness and separateness creates fear. Love brings closeness and oneness, and closeness and oneness bring love. If we could only fully realize that we are not separate. **We are one.** The Talmud, the book of Jewish laws, states, "Who takes revenge or bears a grudge acts like one who, having cut one hand while handling a knife, avenges himself by stabbing the other hand." We are all in the same boat. What we do to another we do to ourselves. It seems that we are each waiting for the other person to change first. However, regardless of what others do, a stand needs to be taken. Martin Luther King, Jr. stated, "The ultimate measure of man is not where he stands in moments of comfort and convenience, but where he stands at times of challenge and controversy." Yes, it requires a leap of faith. Each of us has a choice to make as to which bucket we want our drop to be in. Unless we awaken and bring our dreams to life, all they will ever be is dreams.

Am I dreaming? Maybe, but as John Lennon sang, "You may say I'm a dreamer, but I'm not the only one." I think there are now a majority of us who want to turn this dream into reality. George Gallup, Jr., the noted pollster, reported that concern with spiritual well-being in the past four years has increased by forty percent and eight out of ten Americans are now feeling a need for spiritual growth. This is the time. Now we just need to implement the SOULutions.

I have, as many others do, dreams about what this world can become. I am very willing to give up my dreams, but when, and only when, they have become reality. Create your reality. Use the brush of imagination to paint your dreams on the canvas of your world.

Someone once told me, **"If we always do what we always did we'll only get what we always got."** You have to make a change if you want to create a change. A frequently heard phrase defines insanity as doing the same thing over and over again, and expecting different results. We have been repeating patterns like this for far too many years. If we wish to bring the dream into reality we need to change how we live our lives. It is as if we as a human race have found ourselves in a prison cell. The amazing thing is that we do not have to stay in this cell, because the key to getting out is in our hands. Now is the time to unlock the door, open it and set ourselves free. If you find yourself confused or unsure of what to do or which way to go there is a simple quote that can sometimes help. **When uncertain of which direction to take, let love be your compass.**

It is not just a matter of choosing what is best for you as an individual. It requires looking at yourself on all your levels. These levels were previously presented as the Rings of Life. First, determine what is best for you individually on the "I" level. Then look at what is best for you as the "We" level. This second level is you with a mate (if you have one). Then examine what would be the best choice on the third level, the "Us" level, of your family. Then the fourth level of your home, possessions, pets, etc. Then the fifth level of your neighborhood. You follow this process through all the rings. Whatever the decision is you are trying to make you would, of course, want to use the problem solving approach. So, for the wisest decision possible, apply the problem solving approach for each one of the Rings of Life. This should lead to an optimal solution as to what is best for you on all the various levels of who you are.

One of the difficulties in manifesting a better reality is the view that many people hold regarding change. Too often change is viewed as an event rather than as a process. When we see it as an event we become less involved and are inclined to sit, watch and wait for the occurrence to happen. By contrast, when we view it as a process we tend to become more involved, recognize that we can impact on it by what we do and that we can actually bring the change about. In other words, we become a participant and interact with it rather than sitting and waiting for it. **Change is a process not an event.** So don't wait…create. Again, I feel a need to emphasize that this does not mean that the change will necessarily occur immediately. After all, it is a process.

Certainly, we will run into those that are very resistant to change and to receiving love. They may appear gruff, bitter, prideful, obnoxious, aggressive, shy, spiteful, suspicious or cold. I believe, however, that they too want love, but they have difficulty or are unwilling to express it. The songwriter Paul Simon beautifully captured some of these people when he wrote; "Some people never say those words I love you. It's not their style to be so bold. Some people never say those words I love you, but like a child they're longing to be told." What can we do with these people? Keep giving them love.

It is the season for planting the seeds of love and growth. We need to empower other people to plant their seeds and to begin living more consciously. I can remember reading about a program years ago that was being used in Africa, I believe. It worked on the basis of teaching a person to read and then having that new reader teach another to read. I think they called it, "Each one teach one." We should try to live our lives in a similar fashion in order to create the kind of world we want. Read the wonderful story of "Jonathan Livingston Seagull" by Richard Bach. It is a marvelous story about how an individual creates their limitations with their beliefs, but can learn to remove those limitations and empower themselves and others with their thoughts, words and actions. Jonathan says, "Your whole body from wingtip to wingtip is nothing more than your thought itself, in a form you can see. Break the chains of your thought and you break the chains of your body, too". This is also a magnificent book to read to kids or have kids read it in order to help guide them in their growth and self-discovery. As Jonathan learned, "The gull sees farthest who flies highest."

The answer to the question of, "How much potential do I have?" can be answered by asking yourself the question, "How much potential do I *think* I have?" Because what we *think* we have, or what we *think* we can achieve, is the biggest determiner of what we do have and what we do achieve. Harry Palmer wrote that, **"A limit can be either a frontier or a**

boundary." We get to choose.

The Power of Passion

What can each of us do to help create this new world and this enhanced way of living? First, we begin with accountability. Accountability is accepting complete personal responsibility for our thoughts, words, actions and feelings. It is acknowledging being the source of control of our life and how we react to life. It is doing so without blaming others for our past failures, our present circumstances or any future outcomes. Being accountable means doing our part to the best of our ability. Since we take from the pot we must contribute to the pot. Our individual contributions are the most important step in helping to bring about the spiritual change. One of the ways for us to do this is to find where we best fit in. I have always felt that people who love what they are doing as a job tend to be good at it because their heart and soul are in it. If we could have everyone on the planet working with their heart and soul in their work the effectiveness and efficiency would be remarkable. It's the basis for the saying, "Find a job you like and you will never have to work again." I believe this to be true, so a good rule seems to be, **Let your enthusiasm be your guide.** Find your niche and serve it with all your heart and soul. Follow that which makes you come alive. Make a difference.

So how do we find our job or role if we have not already done so? We should look back over our history and find those tasks or activities that brought us the most pleasure and joy. Ask yourself questions like: What makes me happy? What feels good when I am doing it? What would I do, or do more of, if I only had the time, money, energy or opportunity? Where do my interests lie? When time passes by quickly for me what am I doing? What yearnings or drives have always seemed to be within me? Be aware that there is no lack of opportunity to create the job or role that you wish for yourself. The only lack we can have is one of action or will.

Is making money bad? No, I do not think so. Unless, of course, you have what one of my patients calls a bad case of affluenza. Actually making money can be good, but making money *while* you are making a difference can be great. A lot also depends on what a person does with their money. It is good to keep in mind that, **The more material we make our life, the more immaterial it becomes.** The problem with materiality is that it usually leads to an increased ego and that can be a difficult villain to defeat. The ego steals the humbleness from us. **Where humility resides, so does God.**

A life without passion, not only has no passion, it also has no life. A fundamental step in our spiritual evolution is to seek and find our passion.

Often we are like a blind man trying to find his way out of a dark cave. We can not see our way out, but we can feel our way out. Passion has a purpose. **Passion is God's way of letting us know in which direction we are supposed to go.** So, find the things you are passionate about, act on them and you will move closer to God. If you wish to find God, find yourself. If you wish to know God, know yourself. If you have a sense of the direction you wish to go, but feel you lack the courage to take the first step, then read Henry David Thoreau's words of encouragement. About 150 years ago he wrote, "I have learned that if one advances confidently in the direction of his dreams, and endeavors to live the life he has imagined, he will meet with a success unexpected in common hours."

For years I listened to the arguments of destiny versus free will. Which one is the guiding force or cause over our life? I came to the realization that they both are. They both co-exist at the same time. As an individual in this lifetime, we have the free will to choose what we do. We were also made in the spirit of God. **As the seed of God is within us, so shall we grow.** Being in the image of God and of the spirit of God we have a certain destiny built in. That destiny on its greatest level is to seek, express and be love. In this lifetime it is to achieve that expression through who we are and what we do. One might also say that it is that aspect of ourselves in God that has chosen this destiny for ourselves and therefore, we are the source of the freewill, and if not the source of the destiny, it seems we were at least in on the planning.

Let us examine this idea further. If we can make an assumption that we do not die and that we do have past and future lives, then in those times in-between our lives do we choose and plan what we need to work on in our next life? Do we agree to work on certain issues like becoming more patient, being more generous or overcoming a negative attitude. Do we make an agreement with God on some level? Or does God ask us to serve in a certain role that would help his goals as well as ours? For instance, might we agree to die as a hero saving someone in a fire in order to help another being to understand what it feels like to have someone put your life above their own. This helps the saved person to grow, but the hero gains also because he gets to learn the importance of serving others. A small incident may be a learning experience that helps teach one or a few people. It may be that larger incidents like the holocaust have occurred in order to teach a lot of people to experience the anger, pain and disgust that so many feel about it. It may be an aspect of our spiritual evolution. These emotions hopefully then cause us to change the rules by which we live life on a personal and a planetary level. As a planet of beings humanity can choose to state that it will no longer stand for this type of behavior. If we allow this destructive behavior to continue on our planet it could escalate and become much worse.

It is so very sad and it says something not so nice about human beings, that it takes cruel and devastating events like the holocaust and World Wars to unite people. Why can't we choose to unite because it is the compassionate, just and logical thing to do? I believe that we have the freewill to do it and that it is our destiny.

Destiny "And" Freewill

I picture in my mind two rubber fences that are parallel to each other. They are miles apart and they run from here to infinity. In the middle between these two fences is a set of railroad tracks that also run to infinity. The fences are the limitations placed on us by life, by ourselves, by the laws of the universe and by God. These are our boundaries. In life we can move in any direction we choose, but when we go too far these rubber fences gently resist our pressure and nudge us back in towards the center. In many ways it is like electron particles moving along an electrical wire. As the electrons are flowing forward they are careening off the outer walls of the wire. They are meeting resistance, bouncing off and progressing in a somewhat forward direction.

I see the space within the fences as our free will. We can come and go as we please. We can do what we choose to do. The railroad tracks are our destiny and this is where our passion lies. In the beginning years of each lifetime we generally wander all over the terrain, at times even heading backwards. Typically, we will occasionally cross over these tracks. When we do we begin to get a sense of passion. Something clicks. We experience it as an energy, interest, excitement, and/or curiosity. When we move away from it we may feel a sense of loss or yearning. As we move forward through time and pay attention to our passions we tend to spend more time involved in those activities. We spend more time on the railroad tracks. It is almost as if as time goes on we tend to wander and stray less. We spend less time near the fences and more time on or near the tracks. There seems to be a harmony or synchronicity that occurs when we find our path and passion. When we find it, things seem to click and fall into place. It's like finding our direction home. We will also begin to notice something else that is very interesting. **The closer we stay to our path the higher the level of energy we have available to tap into. The further we stray from our path the more resistance we meet and the more our energy is reduced.**

I believe that this increased energy comes about as a consequence of an alignment. When, for example, the valve in the heart does its job in conjunction with the heart then it functions optimally. In essence, when the heart valve's purpose is aligned with the next upper level organ (the heart), then greater or improved functioning is achieved. Similarly, when the heart operates in coordination with the circulatory system, the whole system functions optimally. When the circulatory system operates in coordination with the purpose of the body there is greater harmony. When the body is operated in alignment with all living beings greater union and agreement is achieved. When all beings operate in conjunction with the purpose of God an alignment occurs that is greater than the sum of its parts. Similarly, when the sun, the moon and the Earth are in alignment there is a greater effect on the heavenly bodies, such as the tides on Earth. It is also interesting to note that there are "Earth tides" which resemble our ocean tides. For instance, when the moon is directly overhead the ground rises about one foot as a result of the gravitational field. **Alignment creates power that is greater than the sum of the parts.**

A person who is unconscious, spiritually speaking, is not tapped into the higher order or power that can funnel energy to them. In order to increase their energy they, unfortunately, take it from others. They drain the energy from others by the use of control, intimidation and domination.

I believe that when we match a job with our passion that it generates energy. We constantly recharge ourselves. We can practically become a perpetual motion machine. We have as much energy coming in as we have going out. It becomes nearly self-sustaining.

This alignment may account for why there is increased happiness, success, power and effectiveness when we find and travel on our path. I cannot help but wonder what the planet would be like, and how well it would function, if everyone was able to travel the path that they are most aligned with. In my mind I imagine it as being like the difference between copper cable and fiber optics. The copper cable functions on a more physical level of matter particles traveling along the wire. There is more randomness in the movement of these particles because they move more indirectly down the wire. Fiber optics, on the other hand, uses light. Light is less physical than matter particles. These light particles I picture as being less random and flowing more directly from point 'A' to point 'B'. I see this as paralleling the concept of the vertical plane of beings. The lower vibrational levels are more physical (STEM) and the upper vibrational levels are more like lightwaves and spiritual. Finding our passion and aligning ourselves with higher levels of ourselves and the UniverSOUL generates energy, harmony and love. This is one of the ways we can help bring about the spiritual transformation of the planet.

Whether we choose to find our passion at this point in time or not, there is one thing that benefits us to keep in mind. That whatever job we now hold, whatever people, places and things we interact with in our life we try to serve them to the best of our ability. When we do not, it negatively affects everyone and everything we come into contact with. It is vital that we help promote positive change in the world on every level that we touch and experience.

What Coincidence Really Is

As we walk through life we are constantly interacting with people, places and events. Patterns occur in these interactions. One of these patterns we frequently characterize as coincidence. Dictionaries describe coincidence as an accidental occurrence of events that have something in common, but lack a causal relationship. I find myself disagreeing with this definition for these events. Eventually history may prove there is no such thing as coincidence. If something is occurring in your life it is happening for a reason. We may discover that if something is recurring in your life then there is a very significant reason why. It is not accidental. Either we created it on our present spiritual level or it was created on the UniverSOUL level. If we did not create it in the present, then is it the result of something we created in the past. It did not just happen. It has purpose. We would be wise to examine the "coincidence" and discover its purpose. You will find that this tends to lead to increased insight and unexplored occasions for creation. **What we call coincidence is simply a door to expanded awareness and opportunities for creation.**

Earlier in the book I stated that the path that leads to the fastest and greatest growth is the path of love. There is a logical reason why this is so. If we interpret the UniverSOUL level as being the ultimate alliance in which we are merged with God, and if we perceive God as love, then love is the highest level there is. Whatever level of spiritual growth we are operating at gives off a vibrational frequency. We can affect this frequency directly by increasing the degree of our love. Whether we realize it or not, we are one with all the love that exists. It is just that we do not believe it, and therefore, chose not to accept it yet. The more love we give and accept the further we move up the vertical plane. The further we move up the vertical plane the more love we have to give and the more love we experience. It is a growth-generating system. This is why it is so important to love and accept others. If we do not willingly and fully accept others as they are, and accept their words and behaviors as ours, then our vibrational level suffers. If we can allow our selves to come from a higher plane we can say to ourselves that on that higher level where we are all one this other being is me also. Therefore, he or she is expressing what a part of me is feeling on some level or in some place.

If you doubt this...try it. Open yourself up. Decide to become more loving in this moment, and the next and the next. Do it. Decide to come from this conscious loving viewpoint from now on. **Positive life changes occur to the degree that we can maintain a higher viewpoint of love.** Open your eyes wider and see the beauty that exists all around you, in all its many forms. If you feel that in your present state or condition you are unhappy and can not come from love because you see nothing to feel loving about, then you may be in need of a faith lift. Do not say to yourself, "I want love" or "I need love." Instead, recognize and say to yourself, "I am love."

Compression or Decompression

On the highest levels of the vertical plane we are fully in the spiritual world. A UniverSOUL. On the lower levels we are more fully in the physical world (i.e., STEM world). On the lower levels we, as a spiritual being in the physical world, are more dense and compressed.

This "compression" increases when we experience the "pressure" of the world. It occurs as we encounter the pressure of stress or anger, for example. It can be pressure from present-time situations, past traumas and upsets or future anxieties or worries. It makes us more solid by compressing us spiritually. The way to reverse this process is to become decompressed. We can do this by various methods. Some are spiritual, some are physical and some are psychological. It may be going to a church, temple, synagogue, mosque or other religious building. It may be finding a serene place in the woods. It may be a room at home where you can relax and do meditation, yoga, deep prayer or so on. The reason these methods and locations can work so well at placing us into a different and higher state of mind is because they serve to decompress us and place us in a different state of being. We are able to more easily relax and achieve a state of love and oneness with others and life.

The use of these rooms, spaces or buildings does not only benefit us, but all those with whom we come into contact. A more accurate description of these places and spaces would be to call them "decompression rooms" or "decompression chambers". If we arrive home stressed from work and have a tendency to take it out on family members we could first go to the decompression chamber before we interact with them. If tensions become out of control at home the whole family would do well to decompress themselves and get back to a state of love. After doing this and reaching a higher level then we can go back to a discussion of the issues or problems. I believe that in the future these rooms will be commonplace and available in homes and workplaces. In the workplace we would have happier, higher functioning, more effective and efficient employees and management. As we decompress we can feel that we are more open to others. I can imagine the signs in the workplace now, "Eliminate stress. Decompress."

They could be rooms that interact with all five of our senses. It may be the integrated use of light, color, images, sounds, vibrations, scents, tastes and touch that assist us in rising out of the compressed state. They may be rooms that are just the opposite and provide sensory deprivation. They could be rooms that provide nature or an outdoor focus.

It seems important to realize that it is not stress that kills us. It is how we respond to stress. That makes it doubly important to put a system in place to deal with this persistent problem. When we recognize our spirituality, live as a spiritual being, and operate out of our spiritual world there is nothing in the physical world that can really harm us.

One of the best ways of decompressing is to shut down the mind and keep ourselves in the moment. Often this seems difficult to achieve because the mind is always going non-stop. It can be accomplished, however, and the most effective route may be meditation.

What other ways can one decompress? One way is that a person can work to stay more in present time, disarm their triggers, come from a place of love and apply the phrases in this book that they have road-tested and found for themselves to be effective in improving their life and increasing their happiness.

I frequently refer to God in this book. I used that word because it is the most common in my own history. I could just have easily used, for example, Jehovah, the Great Spirit, Brahman, Allah, Jah, Yaweh, or so on. I could have also used more secular terms such as higher power, source, supreme being, the creator or the universal being. I view all these terms in a similar manner. There are those who may take this to be an affront to their beliefs. It is not intended in that way.

When I think of religion I think of the story of the three blind men and the elephant. The first blind man feels the elephant's trunk and states; "An elephant is like a snake." The second blind man wraps his arms around the elephant's leg and says, "No, you're wrong. An elephant is like a tree trunk." The third blind man feels the elephant's tail and says, "No, you're both wrong. An elephant is like a piece of rope."

In a similar fashion, each religion often sees itself as the one true way and views the other religions as wrong. I believe that they are all seeing a view of the truth, but from a slightly different perspective. Besides, isn't God really too big to squeeze into a single religion? The bottom-line questions with religion should be, "Does this religion create a better person and a better world and does it promote love, understanding, compassion, and acceptance?" If you are truly coming from love what else could you possibly have but unconditional love for another person or another religion. Remember: **All roads lead to God.**

We all carry the seed of love. When we see and recognize this seed in others we should take the time to nurture it with the water of acknowledgment and admiration. Then reinforce and encourage it with the nutrients of love in order to help it thrive. Let God love others through us. When the world unites it will speak one language. That will be the language of love.

Who knows how high you can reach? Who knows where your ceiling is? **Your ceiling today might be your floor tomorrow.** Henry Ford said, "There isn't a person anywhere who isn't capable of doing more than he thinks he can." Therefore, if you are presently not fully expressing love and acceptance, then make that your life's goal. Life does not have to exist in its present state. Love and happiness can be achieved for all. The sadness and hopelessness that exists in the world can be transcended. **All sadness resides in that space between the world we create and the world we could create.** So, what does that say to us about what we should do? What is the next step? As Marshall McLuhan noted, **"There can be no passengers on spaceship earth. Everybody's crew."**

We should not fear embarking on this journey. We could never be at any more of a loss than Columbus was. There is an anonymous quote that goes, "When Columbus started out he didn't know where he was going, when he got there he didn't know where he was, and when he got back he didn't know where he had been."

One day the morning will arrive. The dawn of a new humankind will burst onto the planet. There is work to be done and we all have roles to play. We can not afford to be lulled back to sleep by the temptations of the material world. There are many distractions, and some things may be interesting, but the bottom line is...they aren't liberating. At times, in life, it may be hard to hold on to the vision, but it's even harder to ignore it. Do not allow yourself to be one of those people who gets a wake-up call and then goes back to sleep. As Henry David Thoreau wrote, "We must learn to reawaken and keep ourselves awake, not by mechanical aid, but by an infinite expectation of the dawn." I have a dream that one day this nation, and this world, will rise up.

The world is awaiting positive change. All it takes is one card to change a game. All it takes is one person to change the world. That person is you. And the key to the door of freedom is application, application, application.

chapter two

"We"

You may have noticed that I have presented the information in this book in the same life-growth pattern that most of us will be experiencing as we walk through life. The "I" (of chapter one) is the individual. It is where we begin in each lifetime following our birth. As we grow up we make friends and typically take a partner, which is covered in this chapter. With this partner we customarily create a family and become parents, which makes up the third chapter.

Now we will look at how we function from the viewpoint of the "We". The "We" is typically our relationship as a couple. However, the tools, methods and approaches on this level are to be used as well, in all relationships in which we interact with another individual being. Try not to look at the "We" as something of which you are a part. If you are seeing yourself as a part of it, then you are not *it.* You are not a part of your second ring; you are the second ring. Think: "I am not a part of the "We", the "We" is part of me.

Let us always keep in mind and never overlook the fact that we are all one. The other individual is literally me coming from a different viewpoint. It might be helpful to perceive the other person's point of view as what our viewpoint would be like if we had the experiences and history of that person. I believe there is a great likelihood that we would think, say, write, do, intend or believe what they do if we had the same past and present experiences of that other person. Therefore, we should neither judge nor condemn other individuals. We are all someplace on the road of growth. Some are further ahead than we are and some are further behind, but we are one and the same, just from a somewhat different viewpoint.

It serves us well to remember that at one point we were not as evolved as we are at the present time. At some point in the not-too-distant past we probably did not have the sense to be able to pour water out of a boot if the directions were written on the heel. (Now don't even think about writing me to tell me some story about how that must have been the start of that well-known eastern spiritual discipline *Bootism*).

Soul-link

In order to create the kind of world we want it helps to recognize the SOUL-LINK between our self and another being. We are the spirit of God. We are linked and united spiritually. We are in the world (the physical/ STEM world), but not of it. Be cognizant of the godhood in each and every being and treat them appropriately. This has never been stated better than by the Golden Rule. **Do unto others, as you would have others do unto you.** We all recognize the truth in this adage, but how many of us truly live by it? To strive for anything less than the Golden Rule is to not be all we are capable of. Our focus should be to deepen our understanding of all other beings, strengthen our soul-link and come from love. When love is not given or received freely and honestly, then it really isn't love.

Acceptance of Our Self and Others

Life presents us with many teachers and opportunities. Unfortunately, too often we do not see through their disguises, for they are often masked as painful, challenging, unpleasant, negative or difficult people or experiences. Novelist Herman Hesse carried this one step further when he so knowingly pointed out, "If you hate a person, you hate something in him that is part of yourself. What isn't part of ourselves doesn't disturb us."

I have previously discussed that, spiritually, we are all one. What is interesting is the recognition of just how close and interconnected we are to all beings on this planet in a more physical and social sense. Researchers have been examining these relationships. Results have indicated that each being on the planet is essentially connected to every other being on the planet by, at most, *six degrees of separation.* Six degrees of separation is the label given to the theory of a person knowing (1) somebody who knows (2) somebody who knows (3) somebody who knows (4) somebody who knows (5) somebody who knows (6) a particular person. The main point of the theory is the assertion that any two individuals are linked by a chain of *no more* than six acquaintances. This would mean that you and I are connected in this way. You and I have no more than four people between us that link us together. The six degrees of separation show us how small the world truly is and it reveals to us how interconnected we really are.

Recognizing this connection, we really have no other choice but to begin treating the other individual at least as well as we treat ourselves. When we ourselves have two opposing thoughts or ideas about something we typically do not beat ourselves up over it. If we are trying to decide which of two cars to purchase or which of two restaurants to eat at we generally do not get into a yelling or screaming match with ourselves. Usually we will either gather more information and then make a choice, or we will go with intuition or a gut feeling. Generally, however, we do not beat ourselves up over it. When we forget, or are not aware, that this other person is another aspect of our self we often treat their opinion as stupid, wrong, ignorant, uncaring, uninformed, bizarre, ridiculous, insensitive and so on.

Unfortunately, too often we hold the position that author and actress Ilka Chase expressed in a perceptive observation. She noted that, "You can always spot a well-informed man – his views are the same as yours." Holding and practicing this attitude damages us greatly. We need to abandon this viewpoint. It creates too much division and exclusion. **We need to treat the opposing thoughts, feelings, words, beliefs and behaviors of others as if they are our own. Because in actuality…they are.** Likewise, when we can all accept the thoughts, words, actions, wants, feelings, plans, needs, beliefs and preferences of all people on the Earth as if they were our own, then we will have unity and planetary oneness. This does not mean we have to agree with all these people or even take on those viewpoints, but we do need to at least *accept* them as we do our own viewpoints. If nothing else, how can we expect to have our opinions respected when we do not do that at all times to other's opinions?

Similarly, it seems that people often place too much emphasis on finding fault with another person's principles rather than living up to their own principles. It is interesting to note that we tend to find fault with a person or group of people to the degree that we perceive them to be more extreme or different from us. So, if you really want to challenge yourself, find a person or group as different from you as you possibly can and try to relate to them. Try to see life from their point of view, rather than trying to create the world in your image. I believe you will be amazed at what you will learn about them and then learn about yourself. One conclusion will likely be that we need to become more inclusive. We need to ask our self, "What can I do to widen the circle?"

If we can bring ourselves to be more accepting of people, we can avoid many of the problems that later lead to the need for apologies and forgiveness. One method of helping to create this has two components: first, is choosing to be open to the widest range of experiences as possible; second is being willing to not use words or actions that another could find difficult to tolerate.

There is certainly nothing wrong with having a different opinion than someone else. It is okay to disagree. In fact, **One estimator of a being's spiritual level is their ability to disagree without being disagreeable.**

Success in relationships, as in life, in part comes from our ability to assume more than one viewpoint. When we are able to assume the viewpoint of another (walk a mile in their shoes) we are better able to relate to, and get along with that person. It brings understanding and compassion and usually increases our affinity for them.

The Hidden Purpose of Relationships and Some Helpful Perspectives

Far too frequently relationships end because the couple was no longer happy. The problem is that on many levels we are taught to believe that the role of the other person is to make us happy, or at the very least, to not make us miserable. It certainly is wonderful when we can be happy in a relationship, however, I surmise that happiness is not the primary role of relationships. I believe relationships are here for the purpose of growth and to help us become more aware. When we put our expectations and focus on happiness rather than on awareness it may be dooming many to failure. It may also explain why fifty percent of first marriages end in divorce. In his book "The Power of Now", Author Eckhart Tolle maintains that, "...if you accept that the relationship is here to make you *conscious* instead of happy, then the relationship will offer you salvation, and you will be aligning yourself with the higher consciousness that wants to be born in this world."

An incredible union is possible when we consider our partner's hopes, dreams, beliefs, concerns, values, thoughts, feelings, wants and needs to be as important as our own. When we do, we see their life as equally important as our own. We need to cherish our mate's best qualities and be willing to accept the others (which doesn't mean they can't be worked on). So, if you want to help a relationship to run smoother: **Enjoy the best and accept the rest (for now).**

If the real problem in our marriages is the other person, then we would expect to see second marriages being highly successful. The statistics show, however, that sixty percent of second marriages fail. That's right, the failure rate for second marriages is even higher than for first marriages. With third marriages, it is even higher. Why? I believe that is because we have not worked on and resolved the problems and issues within us and in our relationships that need to be addressed.

Happiness in relationships is just one of the many possibilities. Another scenario that seems to occur frequently, based on the divorce rate, is unhappiness and misery. Stable happiness is possible, however, by raising our awareness and consciousness and then applying those changes in positive ways so that our partner can raise theirs. Relationships and marriages are contexts in which opportunities are presented for deep personal growth and awareness. It is imperative that we recognize that they are opportunities for growth rather than perceiving them as events, conditions and people that exist to make our life more miserable.

In marital counseling I use a quote by Notarius Markman to try to help people to see that, **"It's not the differences between a person and their mate that cause problems, but how the differences are handled when they arise."** Similarly, we could replace the words "their mate" with "another" because it equally applies to all people. Howard Markman (not sure if he is any relation) reiterates this point and goes so far as to state that *how* you handle conflict is the single most important predictor of whether or not your marriage will survive.

It is often thought provoking and enlightening to examine the patterns of how we and our partner fight. What is your method of winning? Do you try to yell the loudest? Do you tend to cry? Do you employ cold logic? Or maybe you tend to withdraw? There seems to be a general pattern of us taking on the method of whoever was the usual winner of arguments when we were growing up. If, for example, Dad won by yelling, that might be the method we take on. Possibly Mom was oppressively or ruthlessly beaten down by Dad. We may then connect with her fear so strongly that we take on her role as our identity. If, however, Mom won by withdrawing and then Dad would go to Mom and then apologize, then we may tend to be a withdrawer. We need to learn to override this old programming if we want to achieve happiness in our marriage or relationship.

The True Purpose of Negative Emotions

Learning how to handle our negative emotions is a further step toward happiness. I understand only too well that at times we become angry at, annoyed with, or frustrated by others. This is not something to hate or despise in yourself when it occurs. Everything that angers, annoys or irritates us about others presents us with an opportunity to understand ourselves, if we will acknowledge and speak the truth. We are reluctant to admit, even to ourselves, that often times the behaviors and attitudes that we see in others and judge negatively are the same behaviors and attitudes that exist in ourselves. Swiss psychologist Carl Jung observed that, "Everything that irritates us about others can lead us to an understanding of ourselves." It is usually something, or related to something, that is wanting or lacking in ourselves. If, for example, we typically get angry at the slow driver in front of us, it may be because we are lacking patience or lacking in anger self-control. It may also be that we get angry at the slow driver because we have an issue about being slow ourselves, either in present time or our past history. The reason for this is that our outer world is a reflection of our inner world, so that we are tuned in to those attitudes and behaviors. At the very least, this anger, annoyance or irritation offer opportunities for us to learn how to deal with these emotions and determine if they reflect how we want to present ourselves to the world.

When the irritation and annoyance build up to frustration and the frustration explodes in anger, we have missed many opportunities to prevent this from happening. Irritation and annoyance are like the gauges or indicator lights on the instrument panel of a car. They warn us and let us know that unless we do something now we could be experiencing trouble very soon.

Releasing Our Emotional Tank

Imagine your "negative" emotions being inside a large metal tank. As the negative emotions escalate, the pressure builds and results in an explosion. We can prevent most of these explosions by imagining a tap or valve on our *emotional tank*. Anytime we feel the pressure begin to build we do not wait for the explosion to occur. We open the valve a little and express in a gentle way what is irritating us. We release it when it is an annoyance rather than letting it build into anger or antagonism. This reduces the pressure and prevents explosions. Exploding with anger is like having a temper tantrum. We should not like it when we act childish. Recognize though that there is a difference between being childish and being childlike. Childish is a somewhat negative, unfavorable behavior that we see as infantile, foolish and immature. Childlike is a more favorable quality that allows us to get in touch with our innocence, playfulness, openness, trustfulness and honesty. Allow yourself, and assist those around you, to be able to express and experience the childlike qualities within.

When we are in a state of anger we are letting it out and spreading it to people around us. However, if the solution to anger was to give it away then it wouldn't keep returning to us the way it does. An angry person no sooner gives his anger away, than there is someone to give it right back to him. Buddha said, **"You will not be punished for your anger, you will be punished by your anger."** No truer words were ever spoken. Anger takes away our self-control. Each and every moment we spend in an anger state is, in all honesty, a moment in which we chose not to take control of our life. When we are in these states of anger we often say and do things that we would not say or do otherwise. Later we frequently have guilt and regret.

Anger and Depression: Two Sides of the Same Coin

As stated earlier, Sigmund Freud proposed that depression is anger turned inward. He saw anger as changing into depression when it is unexpressed and stays bottled up inside. Well, if it is not good to keep it bottled up and it causes hurt and pain when it is expressed what do we do with it? The answer is to find a balance. The place of balance between the inner implosion of depression and the outer explosion of anger is the action of assertiveness. Assertiveness is the condition of stating, expressing or affirming oneself.

Imagine a pendulum. It swings all the way to one side, which is aggressiveness, or it swings all the way to the other side, which is passiveness. Aggressiveness could be described as acting in a hostile manner. Passiveness could be defined as not initiating an action or not responding to an action with a reaction. Neither will serve you well for dealing with anger. Assertiveness is when the pendulum is perfectly balanced between the two. Assertiveness is expressing your anger, or whatever you think or feel, but doing it in an effective, appropriate and calm manner. There are two primary ways of expressing anger. One is to rant, rave, yell and scream what you feel. The other is to calmly say, “It makes me angry when you don’t do what you say you are going to do.”

Anger comes out of fear and is a physically-based emotion that keeps you bound to the physical world. Anger is an outward expression of an inner feeling of fear. **Anger robs a person of one’s peace, but deprives a seeker of one’s enlightenment.**

It is clearly possible to control our anger. It is not something that just happens to us, even though it may feel that way. Anger is a reaction that we choose to have. What makes me say it is a choice? Because if we choose to learn how to control our anger we *can* control it. Just because it might be hard to control, it does not mean it is impossible to control. It often feels impossible to control because it suddenly just seems to be there. This is not the case, however. If we could slow down time we would see that there is a step-by-step process that takes place. First, something occurs, then we have a thought about that something. We place a negative label on the something and then feel hurt. As a result of the hurt we feel as if we have been attacked and feel a need to strike back. When we have this thought our body begins to respond to the perceived threat. The body begins to tense up and feel more solid, our heart rate begins to escalate, our breathing increases and so on. As we become aware of this process we can begin to change the pattern. We can alter our thinking process and take heed of the warning lights on our body's instrument panel and choose to not go into anger. Instead, for example, we could choose to calmly express our hurt about the something. Learning to express our self without attacking or blaming others can help all parties concerned.

I have always felt that controlling our anger towards others is really nothing more than employing good communication. **Good communication is like good dancing. You need to feel free to express yourself while at the same time trying not to step on toes.** The more we practice these skills the better our expressions become.

Seek First to Understand

Too frequently we demand that the world see things the way we do. We want to be understood, and that in itself is understandable. If, however, each one of us is busy trying to get others to understand us then nothing ever gets understood. What we have then is everybody talking and no one listening. There is a more effective way of approaching the world. As Stephen Covey suggests in his book, "The Seven Habits of Highly Effective People", **"Seek first to understand and then to be understood."** This should be the first step in our communication with another person. Applying this phrase in our lives serves a number of purposes and provides many benefits. It begins by teaching us, and showing to others, courtesy and respect. It often helps us to be less judgmental. It assists in dissipating negative emotion because when we genuinely understand another person's reasons for a position on an issue we are less likely to feel and express such strong negative emotions. It aids us in seeing more distortion-free because we are opening up to a viewpoint that allows us to come from a position beyond just the "I" viewpoint. And after all, it is the truth that sets us free. Once we can understand and assume the viewpoint of another, we are then better able to present a more balanced, logical and well thought out viewpoint of our own. By presenting it with less inappropriate emotion we further reduce the chances of it leading to an argument or to an inability to find a common ground. We become more accepting. We still might not agree with the viewpoint, but we will be more open to others having perspectives that are different from our own. Although we might disagree with what they have to say, we understand their right to say it. This was expressed so well by Voltaire when he stated, "I disapprove of what you say, but I will defend to the death your right to say it."

Understanding is one of the keys of a successful relationship.

Understanding why a partner acts a certain way can at times be difficult to comprehend. That is because hidden within many of that mate's actions and words resides a purpose that goes back to their childhood. We all have unfinished and unresolved issues from relationships in the past (primarily with our parents) that we are trying to complete or resolve in our present relationships. Beneath the scars, we still carry the wounds of childhood. At those times when you or your partner act like a child you are attempting to resolve those past issues. When those issues come up for you, explore them and help your partner to explore them. Just remember to do the exploration from a place of compassion and understanding. Also, before you go crucifying your parents, recognize that no parent is perfect, that they themselves did not have perfect parents and that you will not be a perfect parent either. Imperfect parenting has gone on for as long as there have been parents.

If you wish to understand the pattern of childhood traumas, upsets and experiences better, then sit down and make a list of nouns, adjectives and phrases that would describe your parents when you were a child between the ages of three to ten years old. All of the positive characteristics that you list you would, of course, want to find in a mate that you have chosen. This seems obvious. Less obvious, however, and very often surprising is the fact that many of the negative characteristics, if not all of them seem to also be in the mate that we have chosen. Try this and see.

Why would this be the case? Because we have this unfinished business from childhood that never got completed. We were never able to reach closure on it so that we could let go of it. So what we often do is find a partner with these negative traits so that we can set the stage once more to deal with the situations again and try to change the outcome. We will say and do the things that we were unable to say and do during our early years. What do we do if our partner does not have the matching negative trait we need to help resolve our childhood dilemma? I have even seen situations where the mate tries to do and say things that cause the partner to take on the negative characteristic so that the mate is then able to resolve the childhood wound.

If your partner does not have a particular negative trait that one of your parents had, and you are not trying to give them the trait, then it may be that the trait is not an issue for you or you have already worked through the issue in a previous relationship. Thus, you have already reached closure, which makes it unnecessary to do in your present relationship. This "unfinished business" behavior pattern helps us understand why the woman who hated her father's drinking marries an alcoholic man, and why the man who had a domineering mother marries a domineering and controlling woman.

Harville Hendrix in his wonderful book “Getting The Love You Want: A Guide For Couples” proposes what might be another prime motivator in our relationships that comes from our childhood. You can find out what that is by answering this question: “When I was young what was it that I wanted more than anything, but never got?” Try not to put it into a *thing* category like a horse or a ten-speed bike, although there may be some cases where that might be the appropriate response. When you answer the question, it can often bring insight because what we did not get then, we may be trying to get now in our relationship or marriage. Again, we are seeking to reach closure and get rid of the excess baggage in order to feel more whole and complete.

Mirroring Reduces Distortion

Another way of achieving better understanding in a relationship is to use the communication tool of *mirroring.* Mirroring is when you listen to another person (the message originator) with your full attention, and after hearing what they have to say you do not assume that you know what they said until you verify it with them. You *mirror* what you thought they said back to them to confirm that you got it right. These mirroring statements or questions have prefaces such as “If I understand you correctly you seem to be saying…” or “If I am getting what you are saying it is that…” The originator then responds by telling you that you are correct or else clarifies and corrects any inaccuracies or misunderstandings. If there have been clarifications, you then mirror back a corrected statement of understanding using the same type of prefaces. If it is then correct, you have perfectly duplicated the person’s communication. This method improves the clarity and understanding of an intended communication and removes distortions and potential miscommunications.

Good communication can also be fostered by speaking as a gentleperson. There is usually no need to use force in our communications. There is a phrase I have found to be helpful in our communications. **Speak from your heart and not from your mouth.** And when we speak, talk *with* the person, not *at* the person.

I also try to keep in mind that there are three sides to every story or event. There is mine, the other person’s, and the truth. Understanding the other person’s viewpoint helps me to arrive at the truth.

The Truth about Lies

It goes without saying that speaking the truth is one of the pillars in the foundation of a successful relationship. If we are not telling the truth then we are lying. Lying comes in two forms: lies of commission and lies of omission. Lies of commission are lies where you say something that is not true. This is what we usually perceive of as a typical or standard lie. Lies of omission, on the other hand, are lies where we omit something. It is where we fail to say something and we hold back the truth. We often justify this second one by saying something like, "Well, he never specifically asked me the question." There is a reason why people lie. That reason is fear. **All lies are based on fear.** If you examine this you will see the truth in it. You may say that you can see where most lies fall into this category, but not all lies. You may even give an example of when your coworker asks you if you like her new dress or hairstyle and you are not completely truthful. You may believe that there is no fear involved with that little white lie. If you look closer you will see there is fear. It may be that you fear she could not handle the truth if you told her what you really thought. It may be that you would fear hurting her feelings. It may be that you are fearful of what she will say to you or think about you. It still comes down to that nasty old word fear that has such power over us.

This insight into the basis of lies correlates with what Harry Palmer had to say about dishonest behaviors in his book, "Living Deliberately". He contends that, **"At the bottom of every dishonest act is at least one belief you have about your own inadequacy."** At first glance it appears that a dishonest act is different than a lie. With a lie it seems like it could be a fear of our own or someone else's inadequacy to deal with something. Let's look again at the example of not telling the coworker what we really think of her dress because we think she could not handle it. When we do we may find something intriguing. Doesn't part of the reason why we tell the white lie have to do with our fear that we feel we can not adequately or effectively be honest with her without hurting her feelings? Therefore, is it not our feelings of inadequacy at explaining ourselves that brings about the lie? Interesting, isn't it?

Why People Attack You

Let's consider the other side of the coin. What if we are on the receiving end of what we feel are negative comments? What if we feel attacked, or actually are attacked by another individual's comments or attitude? How is a person to cope with this? How can we achieve patience and understanding? I apply a phrase I heard many years ago that helps me to see it for what it really is. **The amount of pain people inflict on others is directly proportional to the amount they feel within.** When I feel that someone is giving me a little snipe or put-down I know that they are striking out at me because they are hurting a little bit inside. If it is a moderate attack I know that they are feeling a moderate amount of pain. If it is an all-out frontal attack I know that they are hurting a great deal inside. I know that when I myself have attacked or struck out at another person it was always because I was hurting inside. Understanding why people do what they do has assisted me in becoming a more compassionate person. It has helped me to see myself in others. It also aids me in holding my chosen mental and emotional state. And to be the cause over it, rather than allowing myself to slip into becoming the effect or target of their anger by letting myself to get drawn into it. The next time you find yourself in one of these situations, do not buy into the anger and then retaliate with your own because you feel you have been unfairly treated. Instead, acknowledge to the person that it seems they are hurting. Then determine if you need to inquire and see if you can help them with whatever is causing the pain or whether you just need to be a good listener. This is a wonderful way to reduce arguments, especially with our mate or children. Moreover, when we have hate thrown at us, as difficult as it might be, we need to make every effort to respond with love. **Rather than point a finger, reach out a hand.**

In relationships, communication is the foundation upon which the relationship is built. In working with people over the years I have seen many couples that do not really listen or communicate. What they do is just take turns talking. As Margaret Millar similarly points out, "Most conversations are simply monologues delivered in the presence of a witness." This results in either the certain death of the relationship or a lifetime of distance and unhappiness.

"I" Statements and Pattern Reversals

One of the ways of improving communication is to use "I" statements rather than "you" statements. For example, instead of "You never take my feelings into consideration", use "I feel hurt when you don't consider my feelings." This is one way of applying the arm wrestling technique. It allows you to express yourself while at the same time it reduces the possibility that the receiver will regard it as an attack. Therefore, it increases the likelihood of having good communication, understanding and problem resolution.

Far too often in relationships we get stuck in trying to prove we are right. I use a little saying that helps me hold a positive and workable viewpoint. **For making relationships strong and reducing how often we fight, admit it when I am wrong and keep quiet when I am right.** It may be a bit corny, but it is very effective.

Allow yourself to know humility. Be humble, but not just because it is what is expected of a "good" person. Be humble because it helps keep the ego in check, which is a primary source of what creates problems for us and brings unhappiness.

Too many of us have also acquired the habit of being accusatory or saying things in the heat of an argument and then later having to take them back. Even worse is knowing we should take them back, but not following through. A way to help us remain humble is to not let our apology be any smaller than our anger or attack was. I try to live by a policy that a friend shared with me. **Don't let your attack be on page one and your retraction be on page ten.** The more important the news the closer it is to the front of the paper. If the attack was a banner headline, the apology does not deserve less. Understanding this has helped me three-fold. One, I find little interest in attacking anymore. Two, although an attack may still occur it is less intense and typically very rare for me to have it plastered across page one. They more often tend to be on page six or seven (and yes, I know they shouldn't be there at all, but I'm working on it). Three, I try my best to make any retractions no further back than pages three or four. At the very least I place them a few pages closer to the front than the page my attack was on. Hopefully, as I continue to grow I will do even better with this.

The Healing Power of Apologies

When an individual offers an apology it is best expressed in a sincere manner. It clearly should not have other negative attachments to it. By this I mean we should not follow an "I'm sorry" with "but I wouldn't have said ___________if you hadn't said _________." Do not follow "I'm very sorry" with "but you still shouldn't have _________." A person's apology should always be accepted. Unfortunately, sometimes the receiver of the apology is unwilling to accept it or, even worse, they take it as an opportunity to attack, comment negatively or continue to make a point. Receiving an apology should have none of this. The ideal would be to receive it graciously and then follow it with a thank you. A kiss and/or hug is optional. It seems fitting to remember that to err is human and to apologize is godly, so let us recognize their godliness. Accepting their apology allows them the opportunity to correct their mistakes. Secondly, being open to apologies increases people's willingness to give them. When we give people a hard time after they give an apology it reduces their willingness to give them out in the future. In a sense we are punishing them for giving an apology. If we put ourselves in their place wouldn't we would want to have our apology accepted?

Many individuals find apologies difficult to give. They often believe that if they give apologies they are making themselves wrong, which they find hard enough to deal with. On top of that they feel that they are giving ground to the other person. Nothing could be further from the truth. What we sometimes do not realize is that apologies are the key to our jail cell. The truth shall set you free. When we know the truth and do not speak it we are not free. We are allowing our mind, our pride and our fear to control us. We are choosing to be shackled to a falsehood rather than set free by the truth. We do not have to fear losing face or self-esteem. Many of the people I have come to most admire in this life are those who have spoken the truth, and have done so knowing it presents them in a seemingly bad light.

There is, in fact, a fascinating pattern that I have noticed. **Attack others and those others tend to come to *their own* defense. Attack yourself and others tend to come to *your* defense.** So, attacking them may cause them to more deeply entrench their position and thus, serve no purpose at all. Attacking your self, at the very least, may cause others to move away from a defensive posture that may then allow productive communication to follow. If the person can not handle the truth (assertiveness applied with proper "Arm Wrestling"), then this way work as a backup plan to help bring change and movement.

Choose Your Battles

One of the first pieces of advice I give couples is to **choose your battles.** If all you do is fight and argue over every single issue, you will generally find that you get nowhere. The issues do not get resolved because the argument becomes the issue. Eventually the relationship goes sour because all you ever do is fight. If you are uncomfortable with the phrase "choose your battles", then try "choose your issues."

Transforming Demands into Preferences

Select the issues of primary importance and work on those. Then work your way down to smaller, less significant issues. I find that with many issues it is not a matter of right or wrong; it is more frequently a matter of preference. As much as possible, try to create a win-win situation, where both of you feel that you have won on some level. There have been times where, as a result of losing, I have won. I may lose the argument, point or issue, but my relationship has won. "I" may lose, but "we" have won. So in a sense, I still win. When we demand that things must be a certain way or we believe that we hold the one and only right position, then we are operating on only one level (the "I" level) of who we are. This attitude will never allow us to create a happy and loving relationship. The way to assist our relationship is to see our viewpoint as a preference rather than a demand. We will then have a much easier time achieving resolution or creating consensus in a peaceful manner. This is because we will not be locked into our position, but rather will treat our viewpoint as a preference. This leaves room for discussion, negotiation and compromise. Additionally, this approach reduces the disappointment and frustration we may experience when it is a demand that does not get met. **When demands can become preferences then arguments can become history.**

Imagine there is a room where all successful relationships reside. Whether you realize it or not you hold the two keys that unlock the door to that room. One of the keys is to treat your mate just as you would your very best friend. The way you treat your best friend is what makes that best friend relationship so special. There is love, respect, consideration, honesty, openness and fairness. That is how we should treat our partner. The second key is acceptance. Fully accepting your partner for who they are …flaws and all. Of the two, acceptance may be the least employed component to a loving long-term relationship, but the most necessary.

Contract Negotiation

Another one of the essential elements of a relationship is keeping our word. This cannot be emphasized enough. The other person has to know that they can completely count on you. If you give your word, keep your word. Once you have given your word it is a binding verbal contract that you are required to stand by.

This does not mean that you cannot re-negotiate a contract. You certainly can, but only if both parties are willing. **If one party is not willing to re-negotiate a contract, then the contract stands as is.**

At times we may agree to something that we later want to get out of. If re-negotiation is not possible, then not only is it required that we do it, but it is unfair for us to be angry or pout about it. It is not appropriate to go to a party, a play, or the movies, for example, and have an attitude. At times in a relationship we do things that we really do not want to do, but we do it for the other person and for the good of the relationship. It is not fair to make that other person pay by having to put up with our miserable mood because we previously agreed to do something that we now do not want to do. What can help us get through these times is this. **If you can't get out of it, get into it.** Do not hang on to the negative feelings. Let go of them and really try to make the best of it. When we do this, we will find that we actually do enjoy ourselves more than we expected, and sometimes *much* more than we expected. So try to find some things in the activity that you can enjoy or that you can find interesting. If we really can not find anything interesting then let's take the time to relax and simply enjoy the "We" or "Us" time with those we love. If all else fails we can just keep a pleasant mood because that is what we would want if the roles were reversed.

It seems that when two people are honestly negotiating, compromise can be achieved. However, if it reaches an impasse, then one person should begin offering the other incentives to see if an agreement can be secured. If it still cannot be reached with each person offering incentives to the other, then either the issue is shelved until an equally-weighted set of problems or situations come along, or until one agrees to let the other have their way. By an equally-weighted problem I mean that it may take one medium-sized issue or problem and two small ones placed on a balancing scale to achieve a balance with one large issue. You may also simply balance it by waiting for the next similarly weighted large issue to come along. Whatever both parties are willing to agree to is fair exchange. Our goal should not be to win; our goal should be to achieve a fair arrangement so that both parties win. That way we win on the "I" level *and* the "We" level. The optimum would be to seek soulutions because soulutions honor the relationship, and are based on respect, sensitivity and our highest level of beingness.

Sensitivity in our communication can be most difficult to accomplish when we have constructive criticism to offer another person. A wise person is always willing to at least listen to what a person wants to tell them. Also, I believe that before we ever offer it we should ask the other person if they are willing to receive it. Some people do not find constructive criticism constructive. Frank Walsh expressed the essence of it with humor. **"The difference between constructive and destructive criticism is simple; the former is what you give and the latter is what you get."** What a great quote. A splash of truth with a dash of humor.

There is one thing we can try to keep in mind when we find ourselves being critical of another person. Although being critical may say something about the person being criticized, it says ten times that about the critic.

Handling Hot Issues

Questions or issues that are of a general nature can typically be safely asked at any time. I call these *cold* questions or issues. *Hot* questions or issues are those that have the potential to either lead to arguments or to discussions that have a high risk of not being productive if negative emotions prevail. Issues that fall in between would be classified as warm or cool issues. When there are hot questions to ask or hot issues to discuss we need to be more sensitive and proactive. For these reasons, preparation is needed to deal with hot issues. The following seven-step procedure may prove helpful.

The Hot Issue Checklist

1. PRACTICE. Rehearse what you plan to say. Use a variation of the first four steps of the problem solving approach described earlier in the book: clarify what you want to say, brainstorm ways to say it, evaluate the consequences of each way, and choose the best option.
2. TIMING. Plan when to bring up the issue. Would the person be more receptive in the morning or evening? Weekday or weekend? Before dinner or after? Certainly avoid such times as when there is lingering negative emotion from some previous upset.
3. SETTING. Choose an appropriate place to hold the discussion. How much privacy do you need? Would you be better off at a restaurant over lunch or dinner? If at home is the preferred setting then what room would create the best atmosphere?
4. PRECEDURE. Oftentimes in trying to discuss hot issues, the emotion, past history, or baggage the other person brings to the situation prevents a meaningful discussion from occurring. One way of reducing this from occurring is using what I call a *precedure.* This is a beginning or preceding procedure. This is particularly effective on hot issues. A precedure is a process of prefacing or dealing first with the way that you think a person will react and *then* bringing up the hot issue. For example, if you think the person will likely get angry and that it will then result in a non-productive discussion or lead to an argument, it would be best to address the potential anger first. Then explain to the person that there is something you would like to share or discuss with them, but your fear is that they will react with anger and that it will prevent the two of you from having a good discussion. Thus, you fear that the issue will not get a fair hearing. By using this preamble approach you can assist the person in self-monitoring their initial reaction prior

to information or questions being posed or discussed. The idea is not to use the precedure to manipulate the discussion towards getting your own way. Its purpose is to create as fair and impartial an environment as possible for the presentation of the information or questions.

5. CHOICE OF WORDS. Think wisely about what words you will use and the impact they may have. Again keep in mind that the arm wrestling technique is particularly important in this step, as well as in step six. Do not assume that you know the other person's thoughts, intentions or reasons. The only way to be certain is to ask them. Whenever possible, pose questions rather than making statements or assumptions. When you are making observations, use qualifiers. Qualifiers soften. Examples of qualifiers are "It *seems* to me that you *might* be…" or "I've noticed that *sometimes* you *appear* to…" or "Do you feel that *maybe*…" Also try to stay away from hot words that may trigger an immediate negative emotional reaction.
6. TONE OF VOICE. Approach the discussion with a tone of voice that is gentle and calm. This sets the stage for keeping the discussion itself calm. Remember the arm wrestling technique and apply it. Pace your words and do not respond to an urge to rush them.
7. BODY LANGUAGE. Send good body language to the other person. Do not sit with legs crossed in a closed position or have your arms crossed on your chest. Facial language is also important. Try not to appear stern or accusatory which then puts the other person on the defense. Be aware of your gestures and movements. Most important is giving good eye contact. In addition to the words and signals we send to the other person it would benefit us to become more aware of what they are sending to us. Watch for, and listen to, their verbal and non-verbal cues. This allows us to anticipate what might be going to happen before it actually happens. We can head escalating emotions or behaviors off at the pass if we are watching for them. Also, it enables us to know when to soften our communication. When we sense a negative emotion beginning to occur we can deal with it before it intensifies. When a person gets good at this they can often detect the emotion or negativity before the other person even realizes that they are sending out a verbal or non-verbal cue.

Hopefully, these steps will allow you to more effectively approach another individual, not trigger explosions in their mindfield defenses and be better able to create the best situation for discussion of a *hot* topic.

We should do all we can to try to create fairness in our relationships and in the world. Just as important is to realize and accept that life is, at times, unfair. Everyone on the planet has had experiences of unfairness. When we fully recognize that it is this way for everyone…then isn't life in a sense, really fair. Think about this.

It seems that we too often have a tendency to want to change our partners rather than to work on our own stuff. This is probably the major barrier to successful relationships. Here are four areas that you can assess yourself on to see if there is work that you can do on yourself. When the actress Sophia Loren was once asked what makes a successful marriage she stated, "Love, understanding, tolerance and determination." Think about how you are in each of these categories. Really…take a few minutes now and think about it. Which area are you the weakest in? That would be a good thing to make note of, and to consider as a subject on which to work.

If you actually took a few minutes to think about it I wonder what percentage of you thought about yourself and what percentage began thinking about how your partner does in each of these categories. If you found yourself thinking about how your partner does, you may have a tendency to be looking to see what your partner needs to change rather than what you yourself need to change.

The High Cost of Anger

If an angry person will spend extravagantly on self-control now he will save the higher cost of regret and sorrow later. When we are angry with another person we often do not choose the best way of expressing it. It is understandable that a person is sometimes going to be angry, but we can learn to alleviate the anger when it is non-productive. If we are able to just let go of it when it is non-productive, then that is perfect. However, when it is one of those times that we feel it must be expressed we need to find the optimum way of doing so. There are several ways that it can be verbally expressed and these ways form a spiritual hierarchy or order. The lowest level is to yell and scream. The next level up is arguing. The highest level is discussion. At the discussion level a person would be expressing in a calm voice, "I'm angry about __________." This still gets the message across without the need for excessive force. A person may be correct that they have the right to be angry about a particular issue, but that does not give one the right to be insensitive and cruel. Although short-term anger can be constructive if expressed appropriately, long-term anger tends to be very destructive. It can, in fact, become insidious. If you are going to express anger, then make it work *for* you, rather than against you and others.

Aristotle said it best. **"Anyone can become angry - that is easy. But**

to be angry with the right person, to the right degree, at the right time, for the right purpose and in the right way - this is not easy." Anger always seems to travel with his sidekick called "Out of control." Do not allow yourself to be kidnapped by your anger.

It can be a real balancing act for a couple to make a relationship work. I mean this literally as well as figuratively. One issue comes to mind immediately. It is in regard to emotions, and especially anger. Picture a seesaw in your mind and imagine that person "A" is sitting about halfway down the length of his side of the board. Person "B" is also sitting at the halfway point on her side of the board. We might consider this the normal state of a relationship. What you have is good balance.

If person A suddenly gets angry he begins to move back a few feet towards the end of his board and the relationship is now out of balance. If person B responds by moving towards person A's anger (being drawn toward person A's side of the board) then person B is also angry now and it throws the situation and the seesaw even further out of balance.

If instead of moving towards the anger, person B remains calm and moves away from the anger (moves further away on her side of the board) it will begin to bring the situation back into balance. Do not get drawn toward their anger or negative emotion, instead move in the opposite direction. So when your partner is angry, you remain calm. When your partner is *very* angry, you remain *very* calm. If you want to put a relationship back into balance use the knowledge of this "Seesaw Effect" to create it. We can present this as two rules of thumb. **Only one person should be angry at a time** and **When a negative emotion is presented by another, balance can be achieved by moving in an equal and opposite direction with your emotion.** We can actually apply this approach to any negative-type emotion or behavior. For example, we could express it this way: **Be kind to kind people, and even kinder to unkind people.**

It is interesting to note that many people in relationships appear to be poor estimators of percentages. They often feel that they are contributing 50% or more to a relationship when in reality it is typically 40% or less. When this is the case it leaves a gap of 20% or more between the partners in a relationship. If each party would give 60% (or more), then they would probably achieve a 50/50 balance. If you are a good estimator of percentages and you give 60%, then the worst that would happen is a 20% overlap. This would greatly decrease the possibility of arguments because there would be no room for something to fall between the cracks resulting in a finger-pointing battle. Canadian-born author and scientist, O.A. Battista described this problem perceptively and succinctly. He stated, "The fellow who says he'll meet you halfway usually thinks he's standing on the dividing line."

When I think about the concept of us doing our fair share I find myself being reminded of a refrigerator magnet that a patient brought in to a session one time. It said, "No woman ever shot a man while he was doing dishes." I still can't help but chuckle at the probable truth of that.

At times our partners are going to make mistakes and some of their mistakes may hurt us. There is a practical phrase that can help us manage these rough times. I believe that a number of groups, including the Amish, live by it. **Hate the sin, not the sinner.** Although the word hate, seems rather strong the point is well made. It allows us to put the focus where it should be; that is, not on the person, but on the person's behavior. This is the first step to take in the process of healing and forgiveness.

The Beingness Hierarchy

Hopefully, by our communications with others we are able to create positive changes and growth for them and ourselves. What we hope to accomplish is lifting both of us up to higher levels of beingness. These levels can be conceived of as a hierarchy. I call this the **Beingness Hierarchy** (see Appendix: Chart 2). The lowest ranges have a physical/ body focus and the upper ranges have a spiritual centering with graduated steps between the two extremes. The lower ranges are fear-based and the upper ranges are love-based. As you move up to higher levels of beingness you move out of fear and into greater levels of love. The higher we move up the hierarchy the more we quiet the mind. Also, at the top of the chart the person is pain-free. The lower down the chart we are the more we experience physical, psychological and/or emotional pain. As a person who is suicidal or feeling completely hopeless moves up the chart to antagonism he moves out of fear and becomes willing to confront a person, thing or event that creates fear in him. When I use the word confront I simply mean to face someone or something. It is not meant in the sense of being confrontational, which we often think of in terms of defiance and hostility.

Although antagonism might not be a great state to be in, it actually is moving away from fear and, therefore, closer to love. When the person takes the next step up from antagonism he moves into bipartisanism, which is the condition of being able to see things from another persons point of view as well as your own. Put another way, it is seeing the viewpoint of another as being equal to your own.

Notice also that the elements from the lowest level on this hierarchy (suicidal) up to antagonism are more physical-world oriented. Alternatively, the elements beginning with bipartisanism and moving up through universoul oneness are spiritually based.

State Versus Trait of Beingness

We can perceive ourselves as relating to this hierarchy in two ways. One is a state of beingness and the other is a trait of beingness. Our *state of beingness* is that state or mode we are in at any given moment. This can fluctuate and change up and down the hierarchy in minutes or even seconds. It is like the way a mood can change, vary or alternate very quickly.

The *trait of beingness* is more of a general or broad measurement. It is where we typically are located on the hierarchy on an average day in an average week of an average year. A person, for example, might generally be in the *trait* of contentment, but because of something that just occurred he is at this moment in a *state* of anger. A trait tends to be more stable, pervasive and long lasting, whereas a state tends to be of shorter duration, temporary and more situational.

All of our emotions, behaviors and thoughts would fit somewhere on this hierarchy. We can use this as a guide to help ourselves and others to move up to greater levels of beingness. One of the most valuable contributions we can offer to our mate is to assist them, with their permission, to achieve through our support the highest level of beingness they are capable of.

The Beingness Hierarchy also ties in with something I spoke of earlier in this book. I am referring to the part about our spiritual energy having a vibrational frequency and radiating out from our body in energy layers like an onion. The more we move up the hierarchy the higher our vibrational rate becomes. The lower we go on the hierarchy the lower our vibrational rate becomes. This explains why sometimes we can be at a certain level on the hierarchy, such as happiness, and have another person come in to our space in an anger mode and before we realize it we are down at their lower level of anger. Their lower vibrational rate pulled us down. At other times, we might have someone walk into our energy field feeling down, possibly at hopelessness, and after talking with them we have brought them up to our vibrational level of optimism or hopefulness. So what determines whether they will drain our energy and bring us down on the hierarchy or whether we will lift their energy level up? I believe a large part has to do with what level our *trait* of beingness is on. For example, if our trait of beingness is happiness, then it will be harder for someone to come in to our space and pull us down the hierarchy to their level. If our *state* of beingness is happiness, but our *trait* is irritation then we can easily be pulled down to their level because our happiness is not stable. It is more temporary or situational. It is as if we have not fully mastered happiness yet, so we can not fully own it. Much benefit can be derived when we can make forays into the higher levels of the hierarchy, but the value is increased a thousand-fold when we can attain and master those levels so that they become our traits. If we wish to be less affected by the negative energy, emotions and attitudes of people around us we need to operate from the spiritual world, not the physical world. We need to operate from love-oriented beingness levels, not fear-oriented levels.

Spiritually-Centered Love Orientation

One way of helping to maintain these love-oriented beingness levels is to surround ourselves with other love-oriented people who are doing love-oriented actions in the world. Of course, achieving a high state and trait of beingness only addresses our "I" level. We also have to apply the same techniques to all the other Rings of Life. What can we do that will lift our community rings, our country rings and our world rings to higher levels on the Beingness Hierarchy? Imagine a world operating with a trait of beingness that is coming from the highest levels of the beingness hierarchy. An additional benefit of functioning on the love-oriented end of the hierarchy is that these higher levels can impact on our own physical body. It can make us more resilient and resistant to physical illness. This may explain, for example, why nurses who give of themselves and do so much to serve others can be around sickness and illness all the time, but rarely seem to catch anything themselves. So, I guess the lesson here is that if we want to be healthy we need to keep operating from a level of creating and sending out love.

Ordinarily, when people experience a loss they drop further down the hierarchy. Most, if not all, losses fall into three categories, which are loss of control, loss of confidence and loss of a loved one. Knowing this may give us some degree of choice in our response to the situations.

If we will simply apply the methods and techniques provided in this book our vibrational rate will automatically increase and lift us to a higher level.

One of the ways of improving communication with another individual is to find common ground. Too often in relationships people focus on their disagreements and ignore their agreements. We would have a greater likelihood of obtaining understanding and agreement if we followed one of the approaches of Ben Franklin. He recommended that we first point out everything in the other person's argument that we agree with and then point out where we disagree. It is important to note that Franklin used the phrase 'where we disagree' rather than the phrase 'where the person was wrong'. The former is simply presenting a different viewpoint while the latter is making a judgment.

There is a useful phrase that is helpful when giving criticisms. It states, "Lead with a compliment." This is certainly effective in creating higher level relationships, but I would take it one step further. **Sandwich a criticism between two compliments.** It still gets the point across, but it tends to make it easier for most people to swallow. In fact, served this way a criticism sandwich can actually be quite enjoyable.

Levels of Validation and Agreement

Although validation is too often missing in interactions and very often missing in arguments, all individuals need to be validated. Validating a person is acknowledging where that person is correct, whether by the points they make or the intention behind their viewpoint or action. I am certainly not saying to lie to the person and I am not saying to not be true to yourself and your views. What I am saying is to be *more* honest. Be more specific. Fine-tune the truth. Take the time to see what would better express the truth of the situation. I am suggesting that we hold our viewpoint, but give validation and agreement to the greatest degree that we can within that context or framework. Find the balance between not denying our own truth, but giving agreement to the fullest extent possible. This is incredibly empowering to both parties involved. Look at the "Levels Of Validation And Agreement" chart (Chart 3) in the Appendix to get some ideas of the examples of what the levels would be like.

Notice that the upper most level begins with strong agreement and validation. As you move down the list the degree of agreement diminishes. It moves down from strong agreement and finally bottoms out at partial agreement and validation.

During those times when you are not looking to debate a person on an issue, but rather want to validate him or find a common ground, there is an approach I have found to be very helpful. This may be, for example, when you can not agree with a particular point or statement that a person makes because it goes against your own beliefs or knowledge. A person might adamantly state, for instance, that he is going to vote for a particular political candidate. You might not like the candidate at all or basically disagree with the candidate's views. In these cases you can try to go broader (larger) or narrower (smaller) with the issue they raise. You can go up to a broader view and likely find agreement by saying to this person that you think it is great that they feel so strongly about their candidate. This makes it a true statement from you because it is good to feel strongly about a candidate you are voting for. The bonus is that you are able to validate him on some level. Alternatively, you can go narrower to seek agreement by finding a particular point you can agree on about the candidate. This might be acknowledging that you agree with the candidate's belief that we need to improve the country's education system. As you begin approaching people using this broad/narrow perspective you will probably be amazed at just how much agreement you find you have with other people. Plus it can be achieved without you having to invalidate your own beliefs.

Reinforcing Behavior: Simple Yet Powerful

When we interact with other people it is helpful to remember one of the basic tenets of psychology. **If you want to increase a behavior, you reward it; if you want to decrease a behavior, you punish it.** Both are types of reinforcement and both types of reinforcement work, but reward has been shown to be more effective. Reward does not have to mean giving someone a present or money. It can, for example, be a compliment, a look, a smile, a pat on the back, a hug, a thank-you, a kiss or even simply agreeing with a person. Also, there is certainly nothing wrong with thanking someone more than once for a behavior that you would like to see increased and, in fact, it is advisable that you do. So, if your mate did something wonderful for you yesterday and you thanked her, it can only help further by mentioning to her today that you were just thinking again how sweet it was of her to do that for you.

To optimize the benefits of reinforcement the reinforcement should follow the action you wish to reinforce as closely as possible in time. Also be consistent about it. Do not reward one time and do nothing the next at least in the beginning process of reinforcing the behavior. If you are inconsistent and sporadic with the reinforcement it could send a mixed message and will not necessarily lead to the desired behavior. Once the new behavior is firmly in place then you can gradually begin to reduce the frequency or amount of the reward and the behavior should continue. Eventually the behavior will likely continue without any reward.

One further aspect of reinforcement regards where it should be done. Many years ago I heard, **"Praise in public and reprimand in private."** This is very effective and has served me well over the years. One of the greatest gifts we can give another being is admiration. Giving someone true praise and admiration in a public setting can have a very powerful effect.

A large part of a relationship is developing rules or guidelines that are fair. In a relationship I am generally willing to play by almost any set of rules that is fair, equally applied and that works. So, if a husband wants to take off for a week on a fishing trip with his friends, while the wife stays home with the kids, there is nothing wrong with that. However, then the wife has the right to take off for a week also while he watches the kids. If the husband does not want her to, then he can't go either. If the wife wishes to spend several hundred dollars on a luxury item, then the same goes for the spouse. If the wife says it isn't in the budget for him to spend several hundred also, then they either divide up an equal amount or they reach some equitable agreement that is fair to both.

If I get yelled at by my mate for getting a speeding ticket, then I am going to say, "Okay, so I guess the rule is going to be that when one of us gets a speeding ticket they get yelled at by the other person." **If you do not want it to happen to you, then do not create it for someone else.** This phrase also relates to the laws and process of karma and balance. The concept is the same, but from a slightly different viewpoint and that is, **What you create for others, you create for yourself.**

Ending the Ping-Pong Game

One of the best ways of reducing arguments is to stop them when they first begin to occur. This starts with recognition. A typical battle that I hear between a couple in my private practice goes something like this: "Can you believe he said *that* to me?" "I only said it because of what you said to me." "Well, I only said that to you because you got in my face." "I only got in your face because of your tone of voice." "Well, I only used that tone of voice because of the way you were rolling your eyes." You see, this game can go on forever. What we notice though is that it starts out with something as simple as an eye roll and then quickly escalates into World War III. I call this the *Ping-Pong Game.* It begins with a little tap of the ping-pong ball with the force increasing until before you know it you are slamming the ball from across the room. One of the simplest and most effective rules of good co-habitation is to recognize when you are beginning the ping-pong game and stop it before it gets any further.

In relationships, as in life and work, it is important to separate the wheat from the chaff. We cannot attend to everything and we cannot battle over everything. One of the methods I have found effective for helping to narrow down which issues to deal with is what I call *the blip on the screen.* I picture a machine like one of those electronic units in hospital emergency rooms. If whatever happens to me, or in my environment, is a one-shot event and of a fairly minor nature I generally just let it pass. I see it as just a blip on the screen. If I find myself getting a blip-blip-blip (the event recurring) on the screen then I deal with the problem and set a system or procedure in place to handle the problem in the future in the most optimum way possible.

Frequently in therapy I run into a case of what I call *The K-mart versus Wal-mart Trap*. It goes something like this. A wife tells her husband, "Oh, I stopped by Wal-mart today." The husband replies, "Why did you go to K-mart?" She says, "I didn't say K-mart, I said Wal-mart." He maintains, "No, you said K-mart." She says, "I know what I said. I said Wal-mart." He argues, "Well, I know what I heard. I heard K-mart."

I used to get caught in this trap myself. It is a game that no one can win. It comes from having to prove you are right and it usually ends up in a ping-pong game that creates hurt feelings, miserable moods, separation and distance. There is no way to prove who is right (and it really does not matter anyway). Most of us have been on both sides and played both roles at one time or another. When they are talking we think they said it wrong and when we are talking we think they heard it wrong. I learned to not even bother going down either road because it goes nowhere. It is a dead-end street. A better way to approach it is this: A wife tells her husband that she went to Wal-mart. He asks why she went to K-mart. When she says she didn't say K-mart she said Wal-mart, the husband then replies with, "It really doesn't matter. What did you go to Wal-mart for?" She answers, "I picked up that garden hose you wanted" and he thanks her. I much prefer to have the harmonious second script in my life story than the first one.

As mentioned earlier, an area of relationships that is most important to address is apologies and forgiveness. Apologies and forgiveness are the opposite sides of the same coin. Apologies are an expression of regret for a discourteous remark or act. Forgiveness is to excuse or pardon someone for a fault or offense. Apologies are what we give others when we have wronged them and forgiveness is what we give others who have wronged us. Both are essential and extremely vital to relationships because they permit closure to be reached on an issue. Closure is similar to the hands on a clock moving in a circle and going from 12 O'clock to 12 O'clock. The unfinished or unresolved issue, which also helps promote negative moods, causes the hand to get hung up in time. (Remember, that when we get hung up in time we lose part of our attention and thus, become a little less in present time.) So, how well do you think we could be operating in the world if we had hundreds or thousands of these things lying around? Not reaching closure is like the clock hand stopping at eleven o'clock, for example. Without the appropriate apology or forgiveness the hand never quite gets to complete the circle. If we truly care about the other individual we should be promoting their being in good moods and present time to the greatest extent possible and this means freely dispensing apologies and forgiveness. **As forgiveness can heal wounds from the past, so can acceptance prevent wounds in the present.**

Apologies, forgiveness and acceptance are the greatest medicines in the universe. They can heal and cure an abundance of ills. They are readily available and accessible by all people at all times. The power of an apology cannot be overstated. If you wish to increase your apologies to the highest power possible apply this: **The sincerity of an apology can be measured by the follow-up of thoughts, words and actions to repair the damage and to seek to prevent further similar damage.** Let us all be givers of sincerity with our apologies.

The Correction of Mistakes Procedure

It is never too late to give an apology (or forgiveness). Apologies are better late than never, but, of course, better earlier than late.

For many years I have used a four-step procedure that has been very effective.

The Correction Of Mistakes Procedure

1. Recognize your mistake.
2. Apologize for your mistake.
3. Repair any damage your mistake has caused.
4. Set a system in place to help prevent the mistake from occurring again.

Even though we ordinarily find it harder to forgive when the words or actions of someone were intentional or conscious versus unintentional or coming from the subconscious, forgiveness is one of the best ways to reach closure on an issue.

When we are harmed by others we need to realize that they are acting on impulses, and patterns of words and behaviors that come out of the programming or protection mechanisms of their mind. This does not make it right, but it makes it understandable. Forgive them, for they know not what they do.

Think about this. If karma exists, or we are the creators of our reality (or at the very least co-creators), then what happens to us is a result of something we have done. That being the case, then shouldn't we also realize that it is not that somebody *did it to me*, but rather, more accurately, that I *did it to myself*? Therefore, how can we not forgive the other person. We have to forgive. And while we are at it, why don't we spread some of that forgiveness to our self.

Please recognize that forgiveness does not mean agreement. Just because you forgive an individual does not mean you have to agree with what they said or did. Without forgiveness you are both left with an open wound that never quite heals. If we hold on to anger, resentment or other negative emotions it often does more damage to us than to them. With negative emotions we are often re-victimizing ourselves. We allow the other person's action to continue to cause negative emotions and responses in ourselves. (Yes, it's the old dumping on ourselves routine). If we go so far as to try to punish them out of revenge then we are no different than they are. There is a very clear and important difference between revenge and justice. There is nothing wrong with wanting justice. If it is truly justice that we seek, then recognize that the universe already has that principle and procedure built in to it. We typically do not have to lift a finger for the individual to receive justice, be it through the courts or life itself. It is the karmic balancing of the books. Though it may appear that a person has gotten away with something and did not pay a price for their misdeed, that is not the case. If what we really want is for them to learn their lesson, then allow the universe to teach it to them. Seeking revenge is using too much force and it will have a tendency to come back upon you. There is nothing wrong, however, with seeking justice.

In regard to justice, there are a lot of heated discussions these days about capital punishment. Many feel that for the most heinous crimes the perpetrator deserves the death penalty. If we considered this same scenario from a different perspective it may seem that this is an example of the person getting off easier. From the point of view of reincarnation, he simply gets to end this life and begin his next one. A different viewpoint would seem to suggest that the harsher sentence would be spending the rest of this lifetime confined in a prison. He would have the opportunity to spend many years thinking about his crime and the tough consequences. More importantly, he would have the opportunity in this lifetime to learn his lesson and bring about positive change in himself. When given the death penalty, he can make no correction until his next life.

Being the Cause over Self

Each of us needs to take responsibility for our thoughts, words and actions. Too often we are avoiding the responsibility by blaming others. Assigning blame is the opposite of taking responsibility. When we assign blame we are not only judging, but we are allowing ourselves to be the effect of others. When we blame others for what we choose, we are in essence saying that we are not in control of ourselves. Plus, why would we want to get angry and blame others when we do not like what we see in our own life, when life is just reflecting back to us what is in the mirror? That is what life does. It reflects back.

When we are taking responsibility we are permitting ourselves to be at cause over what is occurring in our life. Even if it is a cause we think or wish we had not created. It is like spending time building your life inside a vacuum cleaner and then going around complaining that life sucks. If we do not like it then we should not create it. Not only should we stop blaming others; we should also stop judging them. We have all heard, **"Judge not lest ye be judged"** and **"Let he who is without sin cast the first stone."** We understand this, but now we need to think it, speak it and act it. Step one is to stop blaming others. Step two is to be more accepting and to stop judging others.

We need to examine our attitudes, how we present ourselves in the world and how we treat others. I spoke earlier about what seeds we choose to plant determines what grows. How we approach the world with our thoughts, words and actions are the seeds that we broadcast all around us. When we spread goodwill through humor, honesty, fairness, empathy and love it creates more of it. Think about how good it made you feel when someone complimented you or how good someone felt when he or she received your compliment. How about when someone was honest with you about something even though it put him or her in a bad light and they could just as easily have lied to you about it or about themselves? Didn't you admire that? Didn't it make you want to be more that way yourself? Think about sometime when you were touched by seeing someone perform an act of love towards another. Remember how it made you feel? Every thought, word and action can be perceived as a seed. It grows and it spreads. You compliment your mate, who compliments the clerk at the store, who compliments a customer, who then goes home and compliments her daughter, who compliments her boyfriend, who compliments his neighbor and on and on ad infinitum. When we give a person the gift of leaving them in a better mood or a better place than they were before we interacted with them, that good feeling spreads to others. It begins a chain reaction. You do not have to be phony about it either. There are an unlimited number of positive, growth-oriented or complimentary things you can do and say at every moment in time. There is beauty and love all around us. All we have to do is awaken, open our eyes and see it.

We can picture it this way. When someone spreads a negative emotion around like hate or inappropriate anger I see it as a virus or a contagion. It contaminates. When we spread peace, calmness, support, understanding and love to those we come into contact with we are spreading a vaccine or anti-virus. The added bonus is the wonderful ripple effect that is created with it.

When we act out of love we come from the highest level of who we are. When we express love towards others, we may not realize that we are also expressing it to ourselves and to God. **One cannot love without loving God. One can only love without knowing one is loving God.**

I will never forget the letter I read in a Dear Ann or Dear Abby column years ago. (Note: I have the greatest admiration for what these two ladies have contributed to a better world with their daily honesty, humor, sensitivity and insight. They have helped educate us all). I may have forgotten which column it was in, but I have not forgotten the letter. It was written by a person who had just made up his mind to take his life. He was sitting in his car at a traffic light waiting for the light to change when a woman stepped off the curb and into the crosswalk. She looked over at him, gave him a smile and kept on walking. It so affected him that a total stranger would do this that he began to feel better about himself. He began to feel that life could be worth living and he made a choice not to take his life.

Think of how this changed his life and the lives of so many others. Think about the potential loss and the grief about his death that was not experienced by his family, coworkers, neighbors, relatives and friends. Yet this woman never realized how many lives she affected in such a powerful and positive way with something as simple as a smile.

Changing the World

The woman's action further brings home the point: **Change one person's day, in even the simplest way, and you've changed the world.** The world became a different place after this woman's action. The world can become a different place as a result of your actions.

Yesterday that woman seized the moment. Today it is your turn. You have the opportunity to touch the lives of many people. You can choose to leave the world somewhat better as a consequence of having lived in it. Make a difference. Apply what you learn. Use you thoughts, words and actions to create a chain reaction. We *can* change the world. **YOU *can* change the world.**

chapter three

"Us"

The focus in this section will be placed on family and parenting. Parenting is, as everyone knows, one of the most important and difficult challenges that a human being can undertake. Our job as a parent is to love, provide for and educate our children until such time as they are able to provide for themselves. I believe families function best when they are operating as a group spiritual system. This, of course, does not mean that a person or the group has to come from a religious perspective, but rather come from their heart, as well as their head, and operate on principles of love and the UniverSOUL. It may help to keep in mind that although children's bodies may be small their souls are large.

Family and Parenting

When I think of a parent and child, I get a mental image that I remember from my biology book in junior high school. It had a series of four photos of a cell taken through a microscope. The caption underneath the photos was "How a cell divides." The first picture shows a single cell. The second shows something beginning to separate from the cell. The third shows two similar cells almost separated from each other. The fourth shows two separate cells side by side. I view this as the process that takes place as children become adults.

Anyone who has spent time parenting children or has been on the receiving end of parenting has some idea of the difficulty of the job and many of the problems encountered.

The difficulty begins as a child enters into our world. From the day they are born we begin to teach them and shape them. We let the baby hear our words, see our faces and feel our touch. This is the beginning of the teaching process. We teach with everything we say and do. Our goal, spoken or unspoken, is to provide the child with the skills necessary to survive in the world when they are fully out on their own. We expect that prior to that time of independence that they will be making steady progress on ability, awareness and responsibility. The child's learning comes from the role models of parents, teachers, friends, family and the world in general. This they combine with their own experiences, ideas and beliefs. The resultant combination is exhibited by them as behaviors.

Naturally, when one considers all the input that children get, they are bound to find themselves, at times, in a dilemma as to which course of action to take. Conflict often occurs for children and adolescents when they have two opposing beliefs or observations and thus, they need to make a choice. How do our children make these choices? They learn from their many teachers in life, of course. What do they learn from watching their life teachers? They learn that many choices are made based on hedonistic reasoning.

Seeking Pleasure and Avoiding Pain

The primary premise of hedonism is that behavior is motivated by the desire for pleasure and the avoidance of pain. Children can be expected to operate in this fashion. After all, they learned it from us.

Understanding more about how our children make choices can enable us to provide better parenting and guidance. In order to make educated guesses as to how our children will respond in given situations we need to develop good communication with them. We can closely observe their words, actions and non-verbal cues. It also requires that we attempt to truly understand their pains and pleasures. One important principle is that in any given situation there is a pattern of behavior in which the individual will chose the avoidance of pain or the seeking of pleasure based on whichever one is the most powerful and extreme. If the pleasure is greater than the pain that will be suffered, then the pleasure will be chosen. If a teenager knows that it is wrong to go to a party that his parents say is off limits, but from which he will obtain much satisfaction and joy, he will likely choose to go even if he knows that he will likely get caught and punished. To him the joy of going is greater than the pain of the punishment that he will receive. Conversely, if the pain that might be experienced is more intense than the pleasure that might be obtained, then the individual will seek to avoid the pain rather than experience the pleasure. In this type of instance, the teenager might study to avoid the intense pain of failing a class that would cause him to fail his grade, rather than to go out with his friends every single night for fun and pleasure. So, the pain of failing is greater and more intense than the fun of going out, therefore, he would choose to avoid the pain of failing. As adults, of course we make the same decisions all the time.

If we are in a situation where there are two pains, then we will choose to avoid whichever pain is the most intense and accept whichever pain is the least intense. So, the more that you know your children the more you will know their choices.

Does this mean that we should have extreme consequences as punishment for our children, so that to avoid the consequences they will choose what we perceive as the right path? No. It helps to keep in mind the arm wrestling technique. We do not want to use more force than is necessary to achieve our goals. Use too much force and we run the risk of creating anger, resentment, frustration, revenge and resistance. Especially resistance. Assigning severe, unpleasant consequences and punishments might stop a child's behavior, but it too often also creates undesirable side effects. We can help by teaching our children one of the basic principles of living. **We will be taught by pain what we are unwilling to learn from love and joy.**

We know that if we want to increase the frequency of a behavior we reward it. If we want to decrease the frequency we punish it. Research has shown that punishments do not have to be severe to be effective. The same is true for rewards. Remember that the rewards and punishments should be given as soon as possible following the behavior. This is so that the child will make an immediate association between the act and the reward. Also the reinforcement (the reward or punishment) should be consistent. You cannot, for example, just give the punishment every other time they do the behavior. If you do it will teach them that they can do the behavior and have a 50/50 chance of not being punished for it, which will likely not decrease the behavior, and in all probability will increase it.

What we need to do is build values, morals, responsibilities and sensitivities into our children. To do so, we have to be willing to model for them the appropriate choices.

Punishment Versus Discipline

Many times I have heard adults say that we need to discipline our children more. Too many of these adults use the term discipline to mean punish. If we look up discipline in the dictionary we see that the root of the word does not mean to punish. It means to instruct or to teach. This seems the optimum way to work with our children. We need to teach, and we need to use patience when we do it.

A useful phrase to keep in mind when you have to assign some punishment is: **Don't shop when you are hungry and don't punish when**

you are angry. Take time to cool down, so that the punishment will be fair and just. Tell the child, I will decide what your punishment will be when I have calmed down.

Children are going to make mistakes. That is part of the learning process. There are three questions that can serve parents, and therefore children, well. After your child has made a mistake ask them these three questions. First, what happened? Second, what did you learn from it? Third, what would you do differently if it occurs again? Of course, do not forget to praise them for their solutions. The praise should be sincere and should include acknowledging them for being a good problem solver. This process will help them to program their selves for dealing with future mistakes, will increase their awareness and thus, help them to make better decisions and fewer mistakes. As good parents we also need to give them the right tools for solving problems and correcting mistakes. For this, I would begin at a very early age to teach them The Problem Solving Approach and The Correction of Mistakes Procedure, as outlined earlier in the book. I would use them with the children often enough so that they could readily see the wisdom in their application. The goal is that they will then begin to automatically use the methods after recognizing the power and effectiveness in achieving positive results with their application.

When a child does something "wrong", such as running in the house and breaking a lamp it is important that we do not criticize the child as being bad. A better approach is to say, "You are a good child, but you did a bad thing. You know we have a rule that you are not supposed to run in the house. You broke the rule and broke the lamp; therefore, I have to give you a punishment. Your punishment will be ____________. I also want you to know that I love you." It is important that we understand that the child is not bad. It is the behavior that is bad. It is imperative that we express this to the child. If a child hears that he is bad and begins to think that he is bad, then it is likely his bad behaviors will increase. As the saying goes, hate the sin, not the sinner. I prefer, **love the sinner not the sin.**

If you are trying to determine what to use for rewards and punishments a good rule of thumb is to watch what your kids do with their free time. If they are watching a TV program, talking to their friends on the phone, riding their bike or going to the mall, then these would likely be the items most effective as reinforcements. Either allow the kids to do them (or to do them more often) or take them away, depending on the behavior. I am a firm believer that one of the most effective punishments is time-out. Time-out is a procedure that involves removing the child from a situation where reinforcement occurs. This could mean having a child sit in a chair and not be able to interact with her environment or the people in it. It could be sending the child to her room. If the room has a TV, VCR, video games, or music sources, for example, then this may not seem like a punishment to the child and may actually seem somewhat like a reward to them. When this is the case you then create a great likelihood of increasing the behavior that you wanted to decrease.

Too often because of the hectic pace of today's world, if our children are quiet we leave them alone. This can be a mistake. If a fight or argument breaks out we are there as the authority figure to handle it. If they are quiet and playing together we say nothing. Reward has been shown to be much more powerful than punishment, and yet here we are missing opportunities to reinforce their good behavior. A helpful phrase is, **Catch your children doing something good.** Take advantage of those opportunities when they are studying by themselves or on one of those seemingly rare occasions when they are doing some chore before being asked to do it.

Elevation Conversations

A useful addition to every family dinner or family meeting is what I call the *Elevation Conversation.* This is a time when each member of the family is encouraged to tell some success or achievement they have recently attained or learned, and especially if attained or learned that day. It does not have to be a success, per se, but could be a failure that you learned something from. It can be any gained awareness that you feel has elevated you. It could be stacking six blocks without them falling, turning a corner on a bike and not falling over, getting a 'B' grade on a tough test, not lying when you could have gotten away with it, recognizing the importance of having a friend, learning how to change a tire, feeling good about having apologized to someone or not striking out at baseball. Some might have more than one success to tell. Everyone should be encouraged to tell one though.

Each person present should acknowledge the person's success or accomplishment by giving positive reinforcement either by means of individual comments or a response in unison by all those that are present. This elevation conversation encourages us to take the time to give positive feedback, helps us promote communication, and places a valued focus on increasing our awareness and abilities.

The Responsibility and Privilege Chart

We can guide our children to behave more responsibly based on a reward and punishment system that is applied appropriately. I have created a "Responsibility and Privilege Chart" (see Appendix: Chart 4) that shows the relationship of responsibility to privilege and the relationship of the lack of responsibility to restriction.

Notice that as the degree of responsibility and maturity increases, the more privileges independence and freedom a child obtains. As the degree of responsibility and maturity decrease there is more restriction and less freedom.

I recommend that a parent show this chart to their child and ask the child how many privileges she would like to have. Naturally, the child has to be old enough to understand what is being proposed and must be capable of carrying out the responsibilities. It should be pointed out to the child that their privileges are based on their maturity and responsibility. The more responsibility they take on and handle maturely, the more freedom they acquire. Also, the freedoms need to be age-appropriate, that is, just because an eight-year-old handles all his responsibilities well does not mean that he can stay out until three A.M.

One of the best ways I know to teach children how to make mature and responsible decisions is to have them learn and apply the problem solving approach. This will teach them to consider all possibilities and make wise choices for themselves.

Multi-viewpoints

The optimum end result that a person can achieve in using the problem solving approach is that they will look at a problem and choose their action based on a multi-viewpoint. The multi-viewpoint is the one that is best for all parties concerned rather than just from their own viewpoint (self-viewpoint) or the viewpoint of another (other-viewpoint). When this multi-viewpoint is applied to the problem solving approach *SOULutions* are obtained. Again, also remember to commend the user on their soulutions.

One problem we consistently run into as parents is expecting our children to use good judgment. Most good judgment comes from experience, unfortunately, and too often, much experience seems to come from bad judgment. So, we will be providing the greatest assistance possible to our children if we can help them achieve an understanding of true responsibility. Responsibility can be perceived as having three viewpoints. Self, self to others and others to others. All three are components of love in our relationship with God.

The Elements of Taking Responsibility

We have responsibility for self. This requires us to be accountable to ourselves for our thoughts, words and actions. It necessitates us perceiving ourselves accurately. It demands that we dispose of our excess emotional baggage from the past (i.e., deactivating and dismantling our mindfield). It compels us to strive to further our spiritual development. We should feel individual responsibility toward contributing to the making of a better world.

We have responsibility of self to others. This is to treat all beings with respect and dignity and strive to see others distortion-free. It is employing the Golden Rule and endeavoring to recognize that regardless of age, race, religion, sexual orientation, social status, political beliefs and culture that we are one. Others are us. It is coming to realize that the only way we can truly win is to help everyone to win.

We have responsibility of others toward others. We can impact on how others are toward others. This is especially true in such roles as employer, parent, manager, teacher or public servant. Our goal should be to teach, model and promote others to treat others fairly. We need to encourage communication and understanding between people.

You may have noticed that this book is laid out along similar lines to this multi-viewpoint. First is our responsibility for our own individual growth. Second is our responsibility for our interactions with others. Third is fostering the growth of others and teaching them how to interact respectfully with others.

The Responsibility-Contribution Connection

It is important that we instill in our children a sense of personal responsibility. We will have achieved this goal when we find them making the best choices even when we are not there to insist on it.

Although our children are not actually out in the full-time *work world* they do have job responsibility. Job responsibility has to do with the quality of their performance on any given task. Their primary job is being a student and all that it entails, such as getting good grades, and doing assignments completely and on time. The job description also includes doing their best on chores at home and any part-time jobs.

Social responsibility should also be required learning. This is showing respect, consideration, courtesy and compassion for others. Additionally, it requires a contribution on their part to the common good of all. Since they are using the services that society provides, such as schools, roads, bridges, parks, protection (police, fire, etc.) and so on, they need to give back something. **If you eat from the pot, you need to contribute to the pot.** This is not to punish them, but rather to give them an opportunity to not take these services for granted. It allows them to gain appreciation for all they receive and to learn the joy of giving, sharing and serving others.

It seems that many kids today are either not fully aware of who they are or they have been allowed to lose touch with aspects of who they are. It would be wonderful to see what kind of children we would have and the levels of their taking responsibility and decision making, if we helped them to operate on more of the Rings of Life. What if at an early age our children not only had personal responsibilities to take care of regarding their own body and their space, but also had household chores to do on the "us" level? In addition, they would, for example, help to clean up trash along a roadway in order to recognize the importance of, and their existence on the community or town level. They could donate time or effort to help with a charity on a county, state or country level. Maybe they help gather and ship used clothing to a person or organization in another country who have a need for it. In other words, help them to realize that they live and exist on many levels and that the other people at that level are a part of themselves. Good parenting should include trying to guide them to express each and every level of who the are.

I always recommend to parents that if you are already going to be giving a child something, such as a new toy or going to a restaurant for lunch, then attach the item to a behavior. Do not just give the toy, but look for a recent behavior that was positive and tell them the present was for their responsible behavior. Let them see that with good behavior come rewards.

Giving Choices: Important and Empowering

We should try at all costs as parents to not get angry with our kids for their misbehavior. This does not serve anyone well. I recommend that we keep our voices calm and use a soft, but matter-of-fact tone (remember the arm wrestling). We might say, "If you're going to be throwing a tantrum you'll have to go up to your room. If you stay down here you'll have to quiet down. It's your choice." **Giving choices is very effective because one learns that one's consequences (rewards and punishments) are directly related to one's behavior.**

When you give a choice you also create an opportunity for the other person to employ self-control and self-determination. When choices are given there is also less likelihood of getting resistance. "Do you want to pick up the big toys first and put them away or the little ones first?" "Do you want to rake the leaves today and wash the car tomorrow or do the car today and the leaves tomorrow?"

Making contracts with our children is very important. It allows both of us to know what is expected and what the consequences are. It creates stability in our relationships. Moreover, it teaches us both to be a person of our word.

When contracts are made they should be explicit and well-defined. You should think about any possible loopholes or wording that is vague and could lead to misinterpretation or misunderstanding. A clear contract is an agreement of truth. The truth sets both parties free because you can count on it and this enables you to let go of it.

It is essential that our children learn that certain things are negotiable and certain things are not. Treating all people with respect, for example, is not negotiable. We as parents should feel compelled to instill in our children a respect for themselves. **Respect begins with self-respect.**

One lesson that is useful for children to learn is that of convenience versus welfare. At times, life requires that we have to choose between our own convenience and someone else's welfare. An aware and responsible person knows where to draw the line. The welfare of any individual should always come before one's own convenience.

Triangulation

There is a situation I often urge parents to be aware of in parenting kids. I call it triangulation. (No, even though it sounds similar it has nothing to do with strangulation). If you have ever found yourself as a parent, in a situation with your kids or their playmates having too many fights and arguments, I would look to see how many kids are present. Frequently when kids are in a group of three it can lead to two of them opposing the third. This can, of course, be prevented by simply trying to avoid putting groups of three together whenever possible.

The Three-Step Approach to Discipline

To get children to carry out tasks I believe a simple three-step approach works best. First, you ask them nicely to do the task (and give an explanation if needed). Second, if they do not do it, then you ask them to do the task and give them a preview of what will be added (punishment) to the task if not carried out. Third, if they still do not do it, you tell them to do the task and the punishment also. If the reward and punishment system is used appropriately it will not take the child long to realize that if they wait until step three they still have to do the task, but they will also have some punishment to carry out.

Once the child carries out the job request without needing step three and having to get a punishment, then make sure you follow up with positive feedback each time. As the child improves you will rarely ever have to use step three. You then begin to thin (i.e., give less frequently) the rewards or compliments for carrying out the job. Instead begin to provide positive rewards and feedback for every job request they carry out when you only have to use step one.

The child who grasps the following concept can serve their self very well: **Discipline can be avoided with self-discipline.**

Effective parenting of young children is different than that of older children. With our younger children we need to use more structure and limits, as well as diversion and withdrawal of our attention. With older children we need to set expectations and then explain about the rewards and consequences.

I always allow children (or actually, any individual) to present their case to me. If they think that some issue needs to be discussed I will listen to their reasoning. And I really do listen. Then I make my decision and do my best to come from a position of fairness. Once I have made my decision I will explain it and stand by it. I will not listen to two hours of pleading. I am willing to reopen the case if they have some new evidence to present, but otherwise I do not want to hear it and the decision is final. Make sure the child understands that: **It is okay to disagree, but not to disobey.**

I try to keep in mind that being a good parent is like being a good manager. When a child or an employee (or even a spouse) has an equal or closely equal idea or solution to my own, then I agree to their plan. If it is equal, why not allow them to have greater control over what they do?

As a parent **we must learn to choose our battles.** We cannot battle with our children over every single issue. Not only is this not workable, but it sets the stage for constant confrontation and contentious relationships. It required prioritizing and choosing what we believe are the most important issues. If we battle over every single issue, then the child learns that every issue is equal. This is not the case. Intentionally, throwing a rock through a neighbor's window is not the same as the child frowning when the parent tells them to do something.

This does not mean that we let significant problems go on without addressing them. In some families there are major issues that everyone is aware of, but that are never discussed. It's the elephant-in-the-living-room syndrome. The elephant sits in the middle of the living room, but it is just ignored as if it isn't there. I have met some families that have a whole herd of elephants in the living room. It makes comfortable living very difficult. Avoiding the problem just does not work. It is like having a noise in the transmission of your car and dealing with it by turning the radio up louder.

I feel that many parents may be giving too much to their children rather than having the children earn it. In what may appear to be contradiction, I also believe that most parents do not give enough rewards to their children. I am primarily referring here to social rewards, such as compliments, smiles and pats on the back. I would think that at the very least a minimum of three to four compliments for every criticism should be given. If you feel that you cannot find that many things to compliment your child about, then most likely you are not looking hard enough.

If an infraction by a child is somewhat minor or if the child is typically acting in a mature way (is self-managing and generally making wise choices) I will consider using a somewhat different approach. Remember that the idea of punishment is to teach. If the child is truly learning from their mistakes then a punishment may not always be necessary or useful. I may tell the child, "You broke the rule, and therefore, you have a punishment coming. However, if you give me your word that you won't do it again, then the punishment will be put on hold and won't be carried out at present. If you never break the rule again, then you won't have to do the punishment. If you break the rule once more you will get a bigger punishment for breaking it again and you will have to carry out the first punishment too." It helps build trust and teaches them the importance of keeping your word. A variation on this approach would be to ask them to choose what they would assign as a punishment and remind them that they would have to make the punishment for the second infraction larger. For example, taking one week of grounding now (punishment now) or giving your word it will not happen again (no punishment now), but if the rule is broken again there will be three weeks of grounding.

Another aspect of reinforcement that is helpful to know is that there are four forms of reinforcement. With punishment we can give a person something "negative", such as chores or we can take away something "positive" like not being allowed to go to the dance. With reward we can give a person something "positive", such as permission for a sleepover or take away something "negative" like not having to clean the garage this weekend.

What we are trying to teach children to do is take responsibility for their actions. Kids have a tendency to blame others when they themselves do something wrong. (Wonder who they learned that from?). These are comments like, "he started it" or "everybody else was doing it." We may want to consider punishing stronger when our kids do not take responsibility for their own decisions and actions. For instance, giving them three days of grounding for their offense and an additional three days because of blaming someone else for their own actions and/or listening to someone else's bad advice or influence. It is critical that we explain this reasoning to them. Similarly, maybe we were going to give them a week of grounding, but we tell then that as a result of being truthful to us and taking personal responsibility for their actions that they will only be getting five days. We should explain that when they blame someone else they are reducing their own power by making themselves the effect. By taking responsibility, however, it shows maturity and allows them to be at cause.

Freedom and Rebellion

We do need, as parents, to allow our children freedom and self-expression. One major determining factor for me in this area is whether or not that self-expression is dangerous. Once a cell divides it becomes a separate entity. Our children similarly need to know that they are a separate entity. They create this experience by being different from their parents. Each young generation has numerous ways of accomplishing this. Teenagers establish their own type of music, clothing, hairstyles, catch phrases, words and so on. They clearly want to differentiate themselves from their parents. It seems a necessary phase for them to go through in order to achieve full adulthood. So, if a child wants to dye her hair green, wear some "weird" clothing and such, then I do not see this as a problem. I may cringe a little, but it is a harmless way to rebel. I suspect that if we don't cringe at least a little bit that they would then have to find some other way to be different. After all, if we are fully accepting of it, then it wouldn't be rebellion, would it.

One woman many years ago told me how she had parents that were very liberal and understanding of her rebellion. In a way, it made it difficult for her to be able to rebel. At one point she bought a polyester pantsuit to wear that her parents winced at. Well, that was the clincher for her. After that it was polyester clothing all the time. Since they would not be caught dead wearing it, it made her different and therefore, separate from her parents.

One of the issues that we have to address as parents is how to keep our kids motivated. An article I read somewhere fairly recently stated that it may not be the best move to be complimenting our kids on how smart they are. This apparently can lead them to slack off and not study as well because "they are smart." A more effective approach appears to be to tell them what a hard worker they are. They then begin to assign their success to hard work. Which, of course, then reinforces it and this in turn causes them to work harder.

Giving Children What They "Need"

When I have parents in therapy who are having problems in the family because of being lax with discipline (i.e., teaching) I ask them if they would ever push their child down in the street and skin their child's knees. They, of course, nearly always say, "No." I then present a scenario of the parent seeing their child out in the street and a fast moving car is bearing down on the child. The only way the parent can save the child is to leap at them, pushing them out of the way of the oncoming car, but skinning the child's knees in the process. Would the parent do it? Now, as would be expected, they say, "Yes." I then point out that as parents, as in all of our roles, that there can be times when it may be justified to hurt another. Let me be clear here, I am not talking about and advocating physical, emotional or mental abuse of another. I am saying that at times, coming from the highest level of spirit, for the most altruistic reasons it may be necessary to cause hurt or pain to another individual. Another way of expressing it would be to say that we should keep our emphasis on providing the child with what is needed. In raising our children it is important to recognize that we should not place our focus on giving our children what they want, but rather what they need. For example, do not give them something they want if it makes them more egotistical or selfish. The child may feel hurt that he did not get what he wanted, but that in itself can be a valuable learning experience. Furthermore, if the child has been making poor choices, then he "needs" to have a suitable punishment. Conversely, if a child has been displaying responsibility in her choices, then she "needs" to be rewarded. **Give your children what they need, not what they want.** How marvelous it is at those times when the wants actually match the needs. We also have to keep in mind that the goal always is to empower our children.

The Flower in the Field Story

This is my *Flower in the Field Story.* Once upon a time there were two flowers. Worry Road is a dead end street. One was growing out in the middle of an open field. The other was growing beneath a large old tree. When the rainstorm brought torrents down on the flower in the field, it had to learn how to grow a strong root system to anchor itself securely in the ground. It struggled, but survived. The flower under the tree was protected by the leaves and branches, so there was no need to grow stronger roots.

Then the powerful winds came. The flower out in the field had to learn to bend and to give and take to survive. The flower under the tree did not need to learn to bend or give and take. When the wind would blow the flower would just lean against the tree. It was protected by the tree.

One day farmer Jones came along and cut down the tree for lumber. When the winds and rain came again, the flower out in the field was experienced and well-prepared. It survived easily. The flower that had been under the tree was ill-prepared and was beaten down. Its survival was in doubt.

There are some parents out there who do too much for, and give too much to, their children. You may be doing it out of love. You might be doing it out of guilt. You may say that you want to make their life easier than yours was. You might, however, be doing them a real disservice.

Allowing our Children to Fail

At times, it is essential for our children to fail. If they do not learn to struggle and cope with difficulties now, then later in life when true adversity comes along they might not make it. Learning how to struggle and adapt helps assure their survival. If you think about it, struggling is nothing more than taking on a challenge. Experiencing some failure and disappointment at an early age may provide them with valuable tools and experiences for later in life. **Today's strugglers are tomorrow's survivors.** Failure can be an opportunity to learn how to fall. It is even more importantly an opportunity for them to learn how to get back up. By learning to deal with failure our children can begin to perceive major upsets as just setbacks or delays rather than catastrophes. They, therefore, become more resilient and more capable of bouncing back from a failure. I believe that in the long run it may reduce their likelihood of experiencing serious depression, anxiety or other negative mental, emotional or physical conditions in their future. Secondly, experiencing failure allows them to have compassion and understanding toward others in life who may experience failure.

Failure provides parents an opportunity to also teach our children how to get back up. Remember though that the least is the best. By this I mean that we should not help our children with a math problem by completely doing it for them right from the start. If we can guide them through the problem by doing 1% of it and they do 99% that would be optimum. If 1% does not help we may need to do 2%, 5%, 10% or 20%, etc. The idea is that we do not want them to be completely overwhelmed by the problem, but we also do not want to be doing 1% more than is necessary for them to understand how to do the problem. Similarly, guide them toward using the

Problem Solving Approach (PSA) to find solutions to their issues of failure or struggle.

In seeking solutions to problems there is one guiding principle that should over-ride any decision we make. Any civilized society should live by this and have it ingrained in their children at the earliest of ages. **Take no action that has the sole intention of hurting another.**

Since I am talking about the PSA again, let me say this. I highly recommend family meetings on a regular basis. One of the greatest actions that can be displayed at these meetings is to pull out the PSA and brainstorm soulutions to the family problems. This not only teaches even our youngest kids how to use it, but it shows them that adults also use it. Additionally, by just seeing the PSA applied and being around it, children will begin to program their thinking this way. When a problem arises they will have a good method for making good choices.

There is something to be said for the concept of learning that goes: Tell me and I will likely never remember it. Show me and I may remember it. Let me do it myself and I will never forget it.

Association Produces Assimilation

The more that our children are associated with something the more they begin to incorporate it. This is true of all people. It is true whether we are talking about something positive or negative. If your child spends a good deal of their time with a group that wear a certain style of clothing you will likely see your child copy it. If your child hangs out with juvenile delinquents or drug users you will probably see your child take that same path. If their friends are into computers you can reasonably expect your child to get into computers. This is why it is critical in raising children to consider whether or not they should be associating with someone or something. A negative association is not necessarily a bad thing for a child. If, for example, the child views a negative behavior and sees that it leads to negative repercussions, then it could be a very valuable experience. Associations are especially powerful in a child's earliest years. Observe what your child sees and hears around them. All of this is influencing them in some way, which they are then absorbing and integrating. They are assimilating it. **Association produces assimilation.** How can we use this concept to better our own lives? Think of what occurs when you increase the time you spend thinking, speaking and acting in very positive ways. This draws the positives to you, which then brings about increased pleasure and happiness. Reduce the time you spend associating with negative thoughts, words and actions and you will reduce the negativity in your life.

If you would like to play an interesting game with your children then try this. Teach them to go do something nice for someone and try not to get caught doing it. Do not let the beneficiary of the good deed know who performed the act of kindness. You can also model the behavior for your children. I read once about what one particular family would do. Each member of a family at the holiday season would take some of the money that they would have spent on other members and used it in an act of kindness where they received no recognition from the receiver. On the day of the holiday they would each share with the other family members how they had spent the money. What a magnanimous gesture and concept. It's such a beautiful behavior and loving feeling to assimilate into our world.

The Similar or Opposite Rule

It is understandable that some parents may be using a parenting style that many may view as a bit extreme. Not that it is right or effective, just that it is understandable. There appears to be a pattern in some of our parenting styles that are a result of our parent's style of parenting. I call it "The Similar or Opposite Rule." For example, if your parents tended to be fairly restrictive there is a good chance that you will either parent the same way or just the opposite. So, you might be either fairly restrictive ("Hey, my parents did it that way and I turned out all right") or ("I said that if I ever had kids I wasn't going to raise them the way my parents raised me.)" Many times the best approach is one that is more middle of the road.

Examine your life and see if you are applying this rule. It is not just about parenting though; it could also be applied to any beliefs (political, cultural, religious, etc.) and attitudes. The problem with using the rule in your life is that it may not be a well thought out decision on your part. You may just be reacting to a negative situation from early in your life by either applying a similar negative or else applying a negative in the opposite direction. Keep in mind that an opposite reaction to something that is extreme or excessive can be just as extreme and excessive. In a sense, it is like being programmed. Whatever the cause, at times, it seems that one parent is very strict or restrictive while the other is liberal or permission-giving. With parenting it often seems best to present a united front to our children. So, one parent may need to lighten up while the other parent may need to tighten up.

Removing Parental Counter-Intention

One pattern that creates difficulty within families, and that I see too often, is parents not communicating well and not carrying out what they have said. **Say what you mean and mean what you say** may seem like an ancient phrase, but it still serves as a good guide. Without it, mixed messages and confusion reign. If you are not applying this, then you are creating counter-intention to your own goals.

If you make a pronouncement to your child, "If you fight with your sister one more time, then you're not going to the school dance on Saturday", then you are obligated to stand by your words if they break the rule. *That* is showing that you mean what you say. Too often, however, when Saturday rolls around we feel we are denying them from enjoying their teenage years, or we feel guilty, or possibly a dozen other feelings or reasons, so we relent and let them go. This sends a very clear message to our child, that when we say something we do not always mean it. So therefore, anytime in the future that we say something they may not take it seriously because they know we may not follow through. When we make these statements we should consider it to be a contract because that is what it is, a verbal contract.

If you feel there is any chance at all that you might not follow through on your rule or pronouncement, then I recommend the use of qualifiers. Try using a statement like, "If you fight with your sister one more time, then I *may* not allow you to go to the dance on Saturday." The qualifier there is "may". Some examples of qualifiers are may, might, maybe, possibly, think about, consider, good chance and probably.

You may say that this also sends children a message that we might not follow through. Yes, that is true, but if we might not follow through, then it is sending them a truthful message. Using qualifiers allows us the flexibility to change our response based on their behavior. Qualifiers provide loopholes and give us an additional bonus. The bonus is that when we do say something without using qualifiers that they will take it even more seriously. Qualifiers allow us to have a handy exit and they do not send a message that we do not mean what we say. It is most effective is to use a gradient scale where possible. You might begin with; "You may want to think about your behavior toward your sister if you're hoping to do something this weekend." If you later need to step it up you might say, "If you fight with your sister one more time there's a good chance you won't be going to the dance." If you want to up the ante further you might use, "You will not be going to the dance if there is one more fight with your sister."

Once you have a good repertoire of qualifiers you can choose the one for each given situation that provides the right degree of emphasis and truthfulness. A gold star to those of you who recognized this as an application of the arm wrestling technique.

It has been said that an apple doesn't fall far from the tree. The implication being that children are not much different from their parents. It suggests that we have many of the same characteristics, beliefs and behaviors. If this is true, and at the very least it holds a kernel of truth, then our job description as a parent is spelled out for us. In order for our children to learn responsibility, it requires that *we* show responsibility in all that we do. A billboard sign quote expressed it all: **"Children have never been very good at listening to their elders, but they have never failed to imitate them."** It is necessary that we change our negative behaviors and attitudes and replace them with positive ones. We would be well served to rid ourselves of the excess baggage from our own early years, so that we do not contaminate our children.

What more can we do for our children? We can share with them all the concepts and phrases that are presented in this book. They can be encouraged to try them out and determine for themselves if they work.

Ambassadors of Love

We can choose to be ambassadors of love. We can decide to teach our children how to approach the world with love and demonstrate for them a love for all life. An ongoing process would be to show them how to overcome the negative forces that reside in our minds. **Free yourself from the traps of the mind and you will free the heart. Free the heart and you will find love. Find love and you will have found God.**

When one can apply all the concepts in this book, a realization will occur: as good and effective as each phrase, concept, or item may be, when it is applied as a whole, the results of the sum are much greater than the individual parts.

I spoke at the beginning of the book about the creation of heaven on Earth. That creation has occurred. I can already see it in the faces, the hearts, and the innocence of young children. It is all around us in the perfection and beauty in nature. It is in the people I know and in people like you. It can be heard in the words and actions of strangers. I experience it intensely when my awareness is wholly in the present moment. Heaven on Earth is here. I can feel it. We just have not *fully* manifested it yet. What is needed is for us to completely awaken. **Unless we awaken from our dreams, all they will ever be is dreams.**

We have the knowledge and ability to speed the process up by following one single guideline: **Be what you want to see.**

If you, as an "I", can become awakened…can become more conscious and aware, then you can seek the same on a "we" level. Either find a person who is conscious and aware already, or through love and applied knowledge, help them to become so. Then raise a family (the "us" circle) in an enlightened, conscious way. All of you should then help to awaken and enlighten your community. When enough communities awaken, we will then have an aware and conscious city, town or village. As this process continues we will eventually reach our spiritual evolutionary destiny on the planet. Earth will have awakened. It will be a new and loving world. Your actions will bring about the birth of this loving Earth.

Our greatest gifts to our children are to role model for them what heights can be achieved by a human being and to present them with the tools to achieve, and opportunities to experience, the true and loving nature of humankind and the UniverSOUL.

Epilogue

Recent theories in quantum physics hypothesize that our minds are constructing our objective reality based on frequencies from another dimension that is outside of space and time. We receive and interpret these frequencies which we then use to create the physical STEM world around us. These theories imply that what we describe and experience as the physical or material world is actually an illusion. This hypothesized dimension that is outside space and time, and is the source or origin of the frequencies that create our physical world, begins to sound incredibly similar to a description we might use to characterize God.

Achieving higher vibrational rates by alleviating our enslavement to our mind, decreasing the hold the physical world has on us, employing activities like psychotherapy, meditation and contemplative prayer and/or increasing the depth and breadth of our love, allows us to gain entry to realms of existence that are less dense than the STEM world. Entering these less-dense realms of existence permits access to the UniverSOUL library as well as to souls that have passed over. Some of these souls may serve as spirit guides who assist beings on the Earthly plane. It makes sense that communication with these spirits is possible if we can increase our vibrational rate to levels necessary to accomplish this. If the being that is in that other spiritual realm also wishes to communicate with us they can assist the process by decreasing their vibrational rate. Once the vibrational rates become closer to each other in frequency a resonance takes place that allows communication to occur. Twenty-eight percent of Americans (ten percent higher than in 1990) believe that people can hear from or communicate with the dead, according to a Gallup poll reported in May of 2001. Twenty-six percent of the others say that they are unsure, but won't rule it out. As strange as it might sound to some people, this means that over half of the Americans polled either believe in or accept the possibility that some form of communication with those who have died can take place.

We can expect in the near future that quantum physics and science will be playing a major role in the understanding of our spiritual nature. I am not a scientist and I know very little about physics at this point, but I can see the possibility down the road of science and religion (or evolution and creationism) achieving a synthesis. It is already interesting to note and hypothesize about some of the possible similarities between how religion and science view the creation of the universe.

Let us assume, for example, that there is a God or Creator and that this Creator is omnipresent. This means that God is everywhere, is in everything and, moreover, in actuality, *is* everything. The laws of physics say that all things have frequencies and wavelengths. That being the case then God would contain all frequencies and wavelengths.

We know that when we create it begins with a thought, then a word and is followed by an action. If we let our thinking get creative we might imagine God having a thought that he would like to create the universe. John 1:1 in the Bible tells us that "In the beginning was the word." Physics theory says that a vibration is the source of waves. If God was to send forth "the word" ("And the word was God") as sound or thought vibration it would create waves. Since God is everything and would contain all wavelengths and frequencies, if he sent out this word "God" then it could contain all wavelengths and frequencies. In summary, if God had a thought and sent out the word "God" it would be an action that would lead to a reality. Is this the reality that we experience as life and our world? I can begin to see a possible meeting place here between science and religion or creationism versus evolution. Wayne Dyer discussed the fact that so many of the other names for God contain the 'ah' sound. These include Allah, Yaweh, Jah, Brahman, Jehovah and the word God itself. This commonality makes one wonder about whether each name or sound is a variation of the very same sound. And it also causes one to question whether there is a common origin or source for the sound. In a sense, are each of these names, in some way, different wavelengths or frequencies of the very same original sound? A color spectrum, when it comes out of a prism, contains all the visible colors of red, orange, yellow, green, blue, indigo and violet (each of which has a different wavelength and frequency) and if we go back to the source of these colors we see white light. Similarly, if we were to take these varying sounds and go back to the source would we find God?

Let's look at this from a slightly different perspective. Instead of thinking of sound let us give some thought to light. In the book of Genesis (Genesis 1:3) in the
Bible it states, "And God said let there be light." Again, if God is everything, then God is all light. Physics theory says that all light combined is white light, which is made up of all the colors of the spectrum. These light waves would have been sent out in all directions. Although waves do not transmit matter, they do transmit energy. If we perceive God as pure white light or

having an energy of pure white light, and God puts this light through a dispersive medium, such as what happens when white light is put through a prism, then could it be possible that it was in this manner that he created the universe with all of it's wavelengths and frequencies? When light travels from a vacuum to a medium (like air or a prism-like object) it slows down. This change in the speed of light causes the light to bend and create a variety of wavelengths and frequencies (like a color spectrum or rainbow). Then if some of these wavelengths and energy were slowed down they could become matter. This is because light has the most intriguing of properties. Only light can be both a wave and a particle. This means in a sense that it can be solid and not solid depending on the speed at which it is traveling. Only light can travel at the speed of light and if someone wished to create something other than light then it would have to acquire or assume a different speed. Slowing down the energy of this light would cause it to shift from a wave state to a particle state, thus creating matter. (An intriguing sidenote: David Spangler in his book, "Everyday Miracles", states that creating or manifesting what we want "is the art of transforming a wave of possibility into a particle of actuality.")

Matter can be viewed as being energy that is compressed or condensed. If we have matter, then we have energy. If we have matter, then we also have space and time. Therefore, if we have space, time, energy and matter (STEM) we have the physical, material world.

Interestingly, according to the scientific theories of the formation of the universe, like the Big Bang theory, the universe began as light and some of it became matter. It started off essentially as electromagnetic waves and some of it was converted into matter and matter waves.

God and human beings have no wavelength or frequency, but we do have energy, and this energy has a wavelength and a frequency. As stated earlier in the book, each individual, or rather their energy, has their own vibrational rate or frequency. This frequency is determined by the degree of our love and spirituality, and the extent to which we operate from the STEM world. When people have had near-death experiences many have reported observations that are quite similar to each other. They described seeing a very beautiful, brilliant white light. Were they beholding God? Could they have been perceiving heaven? If all the souls in heaven are spiritual beings at different levels of growth and awareness, then their energy would likely have different frequencies and wavelengths. So, is the white light of heaven actually the combination of all the wavelengths and frequencies of the souls there?

In concluding these hypotheses about science and religion, there is one final thought. If we were able to move at the speed of light we would see that there is no distance or time involved. In other words, light is everywhere in the universe at the same time. When we on planet Earth view light coming from the sun we say that the light has to travel 93,000,000 miles and that it takes eight minutes and twenty seconds to arrive here. From the light's point of view, however, it is already here. It covered a distance without actually covering a distance. It took time, but in reality it took no time. The point of view of light is that all light that is being emitted sees the universe as a single point and all light is everywhere at the same time. If we stop and think about this we will recognize again that the idea of being everywhere at the same time (as well as containing *all* wavelengths and frequencies) sounds amazingly like a description of God.

As we increase our vibrational rate, we become less dense and we move toward the direction of a wave state. We become more spiritual. We become a state of love and this resonates and forms a greater harmony and union with God.

I believe that in the near future we will see religion/spirituality and science (thesis and antithesis) come together in a synthesis. I also believe that this time is closer than we may think. We will soon come to recognize the unity that exists on a grand universal scale. We will experience the amazement, awe and wonder as the UniverSOUL is fully revealed, understood and cherished.

We stand at the portal. A timeless moment in time. One foot planted on the Earth and one in the heavens. Our next step will change forever our lives and the lives of all that follow. I bid thee a joyous journey.

Appendix

Chart 1

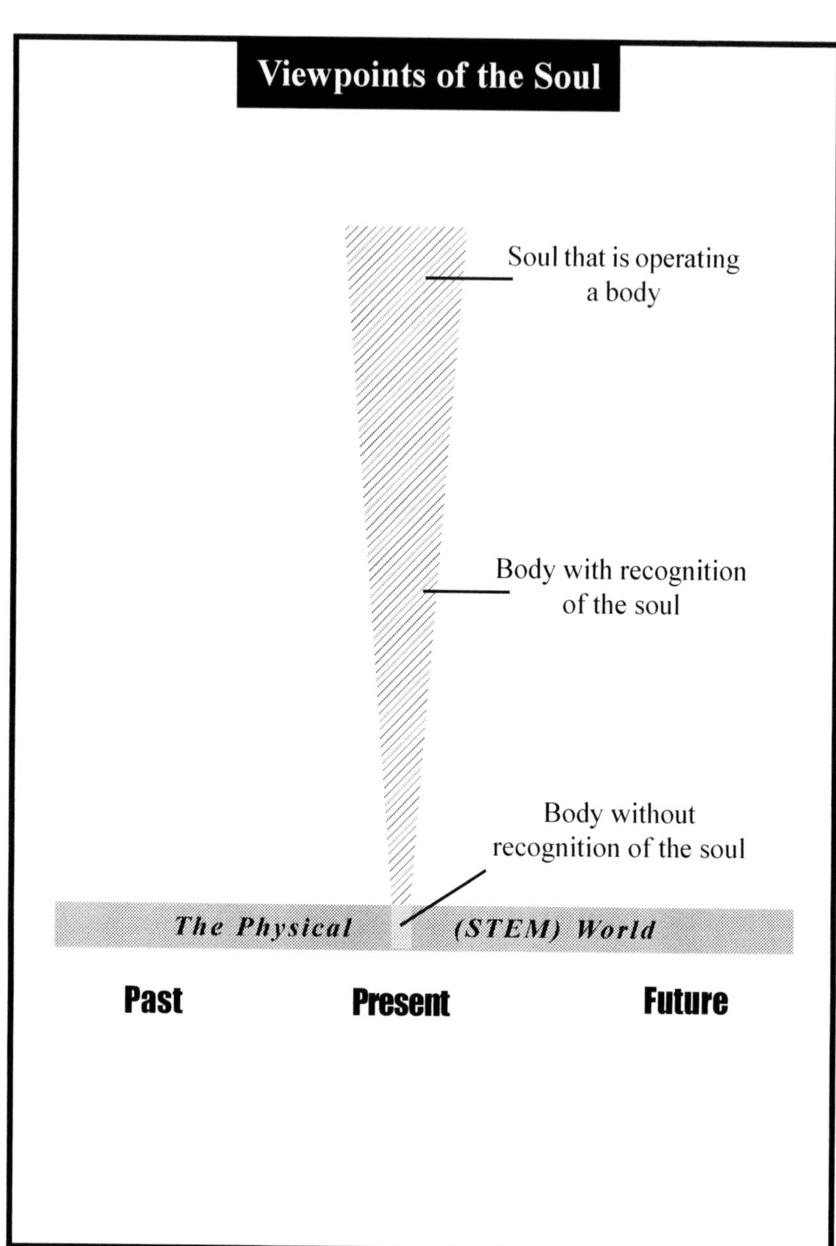
Viewpoints of the Soul
Soul that is operating a body
Body with recognition of the soul
Body without recognition of the soul
The Physical (STEM) World
Past
Present
Future

Chart 2

Beingness Hierarchy

upper range	Universoul Oneness Spiritual Serenity Blissfulness Ecstasy Elation Excitement Joyfulness Happiness Optimism Hopefulness Contentment Satisfaction Acceptance Bipartisanism	Spiritually Centered (Love-oriented) (No pain) ↕ Spiritual
lower range	Antagonism Rage Animosity Anger Agitation Irritation Annoyance Anxiety Worry Fearfulness Hopelessness Suicidal	Physical ↕ (Pain) Physical Body-focused (Fear-oriented)

Chart 3

Levels of Validation and Agreement

Strong validation/agreement

I completely agree with you.

I feel the same way.

I agree with you.

If that happened to me, I would have done the same thing.

If I had that experience, I would have felt the same way.

I feel the same way for the most part.

I pretty much agree with your view of it.

I think most people would agree with that.

I have felt that way before.

I think that many people would agree with that.

If I had that expeience, I probably would have felt the same way.

I'm sure other people have felt that way.

There are probably other people who feel that way.

I'm sure you're not alone in feeling that way.

If I had that expperience, I might have felt the same way.

I can understand why someone would feel that way.

I can understand why someone might feel that way.

I can understand that.

I think most people would understand that.

I think many people would understand that.

I'm sure there are other people who have felt that way.

Mild validation/agreement

Chart 4

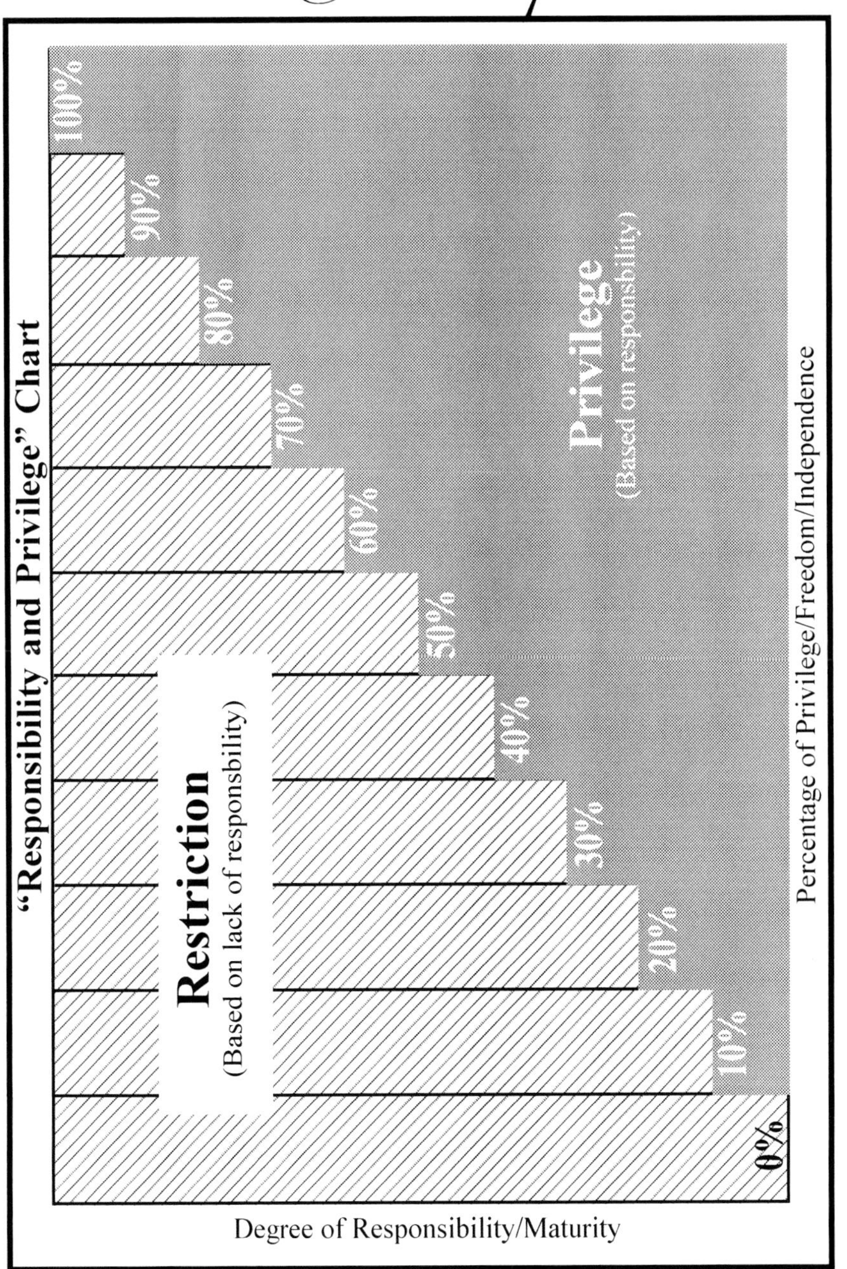

“Responsibility and Privilege” Chart
Privilege
(Based on responsbility)
Restriction
(Based on lack of responsbility)
100%
90%
80%
70%
60%
50%
40%
30%
20%
10%
0%
Degree of Responsibility/Maturity
Percentage of Privilege/Freedom/Independence

Index

Index

A

B

C

D

E

F

G

H

I

J

K

L

M

N

O

P

Q

R

S

T

U

V

W

Y

Z